What We Did in Bed

My Bed, Tracey Emin. Tate Modern, London, 1999.

What We Did in Bed

A Horizontal History

Brian Fagan & Nadia Durrani

Yale UNIVERSITY PRESS

New Haven and London

Published with assistance from the foundation established in memory of
Philip Hamilton McMillan of the Class of 1894, Yale College.

Yale University Press books may be purchased in quantity for educational,
business, or promotional use. For information, please e-mail sales.press@
yale.edu (U.S. office) or sales@yaleup.co.uk (U.K. office).

Set in Janson type by IDS Infotech, Ltd.
Printed in the United States of America.

Library of Congress Control Number: 2019934208
ISBN 978-0-300-22388-0 (hardcover : alk. paper)

A catalogue record for this book is available from the British Library.

This paper meets the requirements of ANSI/NISO Z39.48-1992 (Perma-
nence of Paper).

10 9 8 7 6 5 4 3 2 1

For Matt

Contents

Contents

Introduction

As Groucho Marx once joked, "Anything that can't be done in bed isn't worth doing at all." He was probably right since humans, at one time or another, have done just about everything in bed. For the ancient Egyptians the bed was a vital link to the afterlife, in Shakespeare's day it was a place for convivial socializing, and during the Second World War Winston Churchill ran Britain from within its sheets.

Today, however, the bed has been pushed into the shadows. Sleep therapists tell us it must be used only for sleep and sex. Perhaps because of its current status as "private," most modern historians and archaeologists ignore the bed. Surprisingly little has been written about its history or the many roles it played in our lives. Yet the bed, where we still spend about a third of our lives, has big stories to tell. What our forebears did in bed covered everything from conception to death, with much in between. Given the boundless possibilities of writing such a book, we decided to arrange our beds into a series of themes, choosing the best bedtime stories to tell a new, horizontal history of what we did there.

Sex, birth, death, dining, ruling, plotting, dreading, dreaming: the theater of the bedchamber has provided rich inspiration for artists. In medieval Europe a recurring Christian motif was of the three wise men, apparently resting naked together in a bed, being blessed with divine revelation. Many eighteenth-century gentlemen artists preferred to turn their gaze to naked women languidly lying among confused sheets, perhaps helpless in the face of ravishment by enemies or exotic beasts, like the maiden in Henry Fuseli's *The Nightmare* (1781). When the French artist Jacques-Louis David painted the deathbed scene of Socrates in 1787, he depicted the seventy-year-old philosopher as vibrantly alive and muscle-ripped: the embodiment of principled resistance to unjust authority on the eve of the French Revolution. Then there were images of unoccupied wooden beds, such as Van Gogh's disarming blood-red bed in *The Bedroom* (1888) and Robert Rauschenberg's *Bed* (1955), its sleeping quilt painted with fingernail polish, toothpaste, and paint. More recently, the installation artist Chiharu Shiota has produced intricate, almost otherworldly bed-themed images such as *During Sleep* (2002), which shows women in white nightdresses asleep in hospital beds, weaving together ideas of female disease, weakness, and mythology.

Perhaps the most famous bed image of all is *My Bed* (1998) by the British artist Tracey Emin. In a moment of inspiration Emin displayed her post-breakup bed in all its crumpled disorder, surrounded by underwear stained by menstrual blood, empty bottles, cigarette butts, and used condoms. *My Bed* sparked a great deal of vitriol—not just because people questioned whether it was really "art," but precisely because the bed today is considered a deeply private place that should not be discussed or seen in polite society. Yet such a viewpoint is very recent. In the early modern era, which the historian Carole Shammas has jokingly dubbed the Age of the Bed, the bed was often displayed in the main room for all to see, the most prized and valuable piece of furniture a family might buy. But our obsession with beds goes back much further.

Of our very earliest ancestors' beds we have no evidence. They lived in predator-rich environments in the African heartland, at first sleeping in trees and then, as time unfolded, in rock shelters and caves as well as open camps, huddled close together before bright hearths. But how could they protect themselves against lurking beasts at night? Once tamed, fire offered not only warmth and cooked food but also protected places where people could gather and sleep after dark. It gave light and reassurance in the darkness of primordial landscapes where large animals hunted at night. We can imagine a hunting band sitting around a blazing hearth, the flames flickering in the darkness. Sometimes animal eyes would shine briefly in the gloom as beasts sought prey or discarded bones cast far from the flames. When darkness fell, human life revolved around the hearth and the rock shelter.

The oldest known beds come from a cave in South Africa. Dug into the cave floor, they were left by modern humans around seventy thousand years ago. It happens that the Proto-Germanic root of the word *bed* means "a resting place dug into the earth." This is rather apt, not just because of the dug-out nature of the first beds but also because the bed has always been a place to rest, even though it was used for much more.

In modernity's well-heated houses we forget our ancestors' vulnerability to nature and the environment, but how and where one slept was always crucial for both warmth and protection. In subzero climates like those of the Late Ice Age or of the Canadian Arctic as recently as two centuries ago, people would retire to bed as the temperatures plummeted and the days grew short, virtually hibernating under piles of furs. Sleepers living in winter houses on Independence Sound in Baffinland four thousand years ago spent the months of darkness in a semi-somnolent state, lying huddled together under thick, warm musk ox hides with food and fuel within easy reach.

Millions of people today still sleep on the ground or on concrete or wooden floors, wrapped in blankets or furs or swathed in clothing. But with the rise of civilization over five thousand years ago, beds often rose too—particularly among the elite. In ancient Egypt the dry climate has preserved examples of such couches. By Tutankhamun's time, around the mid-fourteenth century BC, the basic design of the bed (as we would recognize it) was well established, albeit slightly higher at the pillow end and with a footboard to prevent the sleeper from sliding off. There might seem to be few variations on the theme of a sleeping platform, but as we dig deeper we find more. There were cupboard beds and hammocks, low waterbeds and high beds sixteen feet off the floor. Nonetheless, the basic rectangular design has changed remarkably little over the past five thousand years. Even mattresses have hardly changed over the millennia. Grass, hay, and straw stuffed into sacks or cloth bags served as the basic mattress for centuries. Those who could afford it slept on multiple layers to avoid the bugs and scratchiness of the stuffing. The great elaboration of sleeping technology is a product of the current century, with tricks and quackery to combat insomnia.

A huge body of research surrounds sleep and its evolutionary history, especially a practice known as segmented sleep that seems to have been commonplace before electric light turned night into day. People slept for, say, four hours, after which they would awaken and spend time having sex, analyzing dreams, praying, doing chores, meeting friends, or committing crimes and other devilish deeds, and then return to bed for another four hours or so. As recently as the seventeenth century, London streets echoed to the sound of merchants touting their wares at 3:00 a.m., which suggests there must have been willing customers at that hour. Perhaps, think some, it is our modern desire to deny this "natural" sleep rhythm that has led to our current multibillion-dollar reliance on sleeping pills. Could we solve our sleep problems simply by understanding how we used to do things?

Aside from sleep, much else went on in bed. Depending on the cultural mores, it was often a platform for sex. But who slept with whom, when, and how varied from society to society. Though Princes William or Harry might recoil at the thought, royal sex was often carefully orchestrated. Scribes kept records of pharaohs' and Chinese emperors' sex lives. Outside the palace, sex could be much more freewheeling even if condemned by religious authorities, who cast an especially disapproving eye on anything that contravened the rule book.

We also tend to forget just how important talk was in societies that lacked writing, where everything was passed from one generation to the next by word of mouth. Dark winter nights were a time for elders and shamans to tell stories, recite chants, invoke supernatural mysteries. The tales might be familiar and often repeated, but they explained the cosmos and where people came from as well as their relationships to the powerful forces of the mystic and natural worlds. Time spent in bed was often a glue that brought people together to love and to learn. Where one slept and spent time was central to one's existence.

For most of human history, privacy as we know it did not exist. Bedmates were many, as they provided security. Children, parents, even entire houses or kin-groups would bed down together. The social norms of the bed were flexible and constantly changing. Bed companions could change from one night to the next. Bed sharing with strangers was very much part of traveling, whether by land or by sea, right into the nineteenth century in both Europe and America, and in some countries it still continues. Inns rented beds for one person or charged travelers by the body to occupy a common one. This bedmate arrangement could provide little serenity. The sixteenth-century English poet Andrew Barclay complained, "Some buck and some babble, some commeth drunk to bed."

The bedroom as a separate chamber was once a symbol of royalty and nobility, but even then it often served as a public stage. King Louis XIV of France governed the country and conducted affairs of state from his bed. Only during the past two centuries have we commoners walled off the bedroom and made it a totally private place. Even that privacy is breaking down in the futuristic connected bed, which links you seamlessly to the electronic realm. Until the Industrial Revolution and even beyond, beds were both a pragmatic and symbolic place, a prop, as it were, for the theater of life.

And what a stage they have been! Life usually begins and generally ends on a bed. In the case of royal births and deaths the stakes were high, especially when the succession was in doubt, as it often was in times when life expectancy was short and a monarch could die with little warning. Chinese and Indian emperors routinely slept in carefully guarded isolation, as did Elizabeth I of England and Egyptian pharaohs. The births and deaths of the eminent unfolded before witnesses. Britain's home secretary attended royal births until the birth of Prince Charles in 1948, when the practice was discontinued. Forty-two eminent public figures verified the birth of King James II's son at St James's Palace in 1688, an event which a Cambridge historian has called the first media circus surrounding a royal birth.

Deathbeds, too, often had symbolic importance, as did funerary couches. At Berel in Kazakhstan a Mongolian mound dating to 200 BC held the bodies of two Scythian nobles on fine raised wooden beds. Outside their burial chambers lay eleven horses on a birch bark "bed," saddles and harnesses intact. The imagery is closely linked to Mongolian religious beliefs in a sky god mounted on a horse, symbol of a world where survival and leadership depended on horse-powered mobility. In the afterlife these chieftains would have been powerless without their stallions.

By Victorian times meeting around the deathbed was still an important ritual, though bedchamber socializing was now frowned upon. Separation of men and women was pursued with fanatical intensity, particularly among the new urban middle class. For them, the bedroom had become a private refuge, an ideal that has since swept through the West. For the first time in centuries the basic technology of the bed also began to change. Beds became more elaborate, with metal coil springs coming into use after 1826, replacing the traditional straps or cords. Machine-spun cotton bedding, a product of the Industrial Revolution, became the staple of the well-equipped Victorian linen closet. Great care was needed to keep this bedding fresh and dry in an era of pervasive damp and the accompanying fear of tuberculosis. A Victorian housewife complained that servants never made beds properly. Their first idea was to cover it up, which made it "stuffy and disagreeable." Modern experiments have shown that it would take a servant at least half an hour to make a Victorian bed properly. But it was not until the 1970s that the greatest revolution in bed making occurred: the invention of the duvet, which banished the endless work of changing and cleaning blankets, top and bottom sheets, and other layers of bedding.

Today, the state-of-the-art bed is a mirror of our increasingly technological and multitasking postindustrial society. It comes complete with USB ports and other devices to keep its occupant connected. Meanwhile, rising urban populations and sky-high real estate prices are causing millions of people to live in condominiums, in cramped one-room apartments, and in crowded high-rise buildings. The bed either folds away into the wall or else has reemerged in the home's public spaces.

This book pulls back the covers that now shroud the bed, that most fundamental of human technologies. It lays bare the often strange, sometimes comical, and always compelling history of one of humanity's most overlooked artifacts. From bawdy bedmates frolicking in great medieval halls to the sleeping habits of American presidents, we investigate the complex variations on a little-explored venue and everything people did there.

ONE

Beds Laid Bare

"From nearly all social history and biography, one-third of the story is missing." So wrote the architectural painter and furniture expert Lawrence Wright in the 1960s, while reflecting on the bed-shaped gap in our understanding of the past.[1] Beds are missing from most of archaeology, too. But if one digs, one finds, and for us, as archaeologists, the bed as artifact is the logical place to start our horizontal history.

THE URGE TO BED DOWN

The point at which we humans first used beds depends on how you define one. Our ancient ancestors probably slept high above the ground, much like our still-living primate relatives, perhaps in bundles of branches and grass. We had to: the landscapes of our East African homeland teemed with dangerous animals that considered us lunch. Bedding down aloft worked well for the millions of years during which our forebears thrived without the protection of fire or efficient hunting weapons. Most vulnerable when they were asleep or nursing their young, they looked for resting places on stiff branches with good bending strength and perhaps constructed nests of grass and leaves. These treetop beds have, of course, long been lost to time.

Our closest living relative, the chimpanzee, gives us an insight into how we might have made our beds. In the Toro-Semliki Reserve of western Uganda chimps use the branches of the Ugandan ironwood, a tree with strong, widely spaced limbs, to weave the shoots together to make durable beds.[2] Other chimpanzee populations also choose their nest materials carefully, and most make a new bed daily. This means their beds are surprisingly clean, harboring far fewer fecal and skin bacteria than are found in the average human bed.[3] We can be sure that our remote ancestors did just the same. High above the ground, they must have used their nests for sleeping, resting during the heat of the day, and breeding. No human beings now sleep habitually in tree nests.

About two million years ago—the date is still debated—our forebears tamed fire. Fire provided warmth, allowed people to cook, and, above all, gave protection from beasts. Once they had fire, our ancestors began to sleep on the ground, around hearths in open-air camps, under rocky overhangs or in caves. Fire enhanced food sharing, and its seductive warmth caused people to huddle together, helping to forge close relationships among small human bands. Home bases and family ties became more important. Relationships between men and women must have changed profoundly. Proximity to the fire and close physical contact night after night helped turn sexual relationships from opportunistic encounters into habitual sex with the same partner(s) in shared sleeping places. Pair bonding may be a recent feature in human evolution, and it's intriguing to imagine that technology—fire and the bed—played a role in its emergence. The bed, perhaps little more than a pile of grass or a hide, became central to daily life, an important focus not just of sleep but also of day-to-day sharing and grooming.

Much of this description of our earliest behavior is informed conjecture. It's only with archaeology's oldest known beds that we have some concrete evidence of what we used to do. These beds come from Sibudu rock shelter in a cliff above the uThongathi River in South Africa, forty kilometers north of Durban and fifteen kilometers from the Indian Ocean.[4] Modern people, *Homo sapiens*, who were physically and no doubt mentally just like ourselves, visited the shelter at least fifteen times between about seventy-seven thousand and thirty-eight thousand years ago and slept there. Thick swaths of grasses, sedges, and rushes that still grow by the nearby river tell a story of regular but careful slumber. Anyone who sleeps in a cave or rock shelter finds it hard to keep it clean and free of insects, but the Sibudu people were experts at it. They defended themselves with the aromatic leaves of *Cryptocraya woodii*, the Cape laurel tree, which contain several chemical compounds that can kill insects and repel mosquitoes and other pests. The sleepers also burned their bedding regularly to get rid of insects and garbage, then laid fresh grass and rushes to make new beds. They seem to have liked king-sized beds. Most of the bedding covers at least three well-trodden square meters. These were far more than sleeping places. People prepared food and ate it while lounging on the grass, and it appears they liked to combine activities.

Fifty thousand years ago our Neanderthal cousins at Esquilleu cave, southwest of Santander in northern Spain, also slept on piles of grass. Twenty-three thousand years later our direct ancestors occupied a hunting and fishing camp, known as Ohalo II, on the shores of the Sea of Galilee in Israel.[5] The submerged encampment, exposed by the falling lake level, yielded an oval-shaped hut floor covered with carefully placed lakeside grasses with soft, delicate stems. Those who collected them cut the stems with sharp-edged stone tools and arranged them tightly on the ground. Then they laid down a compact layer of clay to protect the grass and form a simple, thin mat. The soft grass layer was a good place to sleep. The sleepers arranged the grass bunches like tiles near the walls, leaving an open space in the center for the hearth. The Ohalo people's bedding was quite sophisticated. Simple layers of grass around the central hearth and the entrance served for food preparation and tool manufacture. No prehistoric bed-and-breakfast this, but a place where people took nighttime comfort seriously. Sleeping places were apart, as they are in modern hunting camps.

For thousands of years people slept cheek by jowl, close to fires and crammed together for warmth, in colder climates buried under furs and hides. Warmth and protection were the sleeper's primordial needs. Privacy was unknown: people paired off, had babies, breast-fed them, became ill or died, all within arm's-reach of their kin. Only a few places remind us of this reality, among them Hinds Cave in eastern Texas, which lies in a tributary canyon of the Pecos River.[6] People first visited the cave as early as 7000 BC. Three meters (9.8 feet) of dry cave fill are an archaeological treasure trove, preserving everything from plants to mats, baskets, and bedding. Groups of ten to fifteen people visited the cave and used it in much the same way for thousands of years. Two areas, one at the back of the cave, another in a side alcove, yielded the remains of grass-lined sleeping pits and hearths. A large latrine area lay between the two sleeping areas. To make their beds, the visitors dug shallow pits and lined them with small, leafy branches. Then came a well-padded layer of woven mat fragments, sometimes discarded sandals, topped by a soft grass fill and a sleeping mat. Snug they must have been, for the pits were about 0.9 meter long and 0.6 meter across. These were sleeping places, unwieldy for anything else. Those who used them must have slept in a crouched position, perhaps to conserve body heat.

SLEEPING WITH THE ANCESTORS

Fast forward to 3200 BC to the southern shores of the Bay o'Skaill in Britain's Orkney Islands. The bay is a tempestuous, windy place. A great storm in 1850 brought exceptionally high tides and a gale that stripped the grass from a mound known as Skerrabra (in modern spelling, Skara Brae), revealing the outlines of ancient stone buildings. The local laird, William Watt of Skaill, dug out four houses and then stopped work. Nothing more happened until 1925, when another fierce tempest damaged some of the dwellings. The locals built a seawall to preserve the structures and in the process found more houses. Between 1928 and 1930 Vere Gordon Childe of Edinburgh University, one of the most eminent archaeologists of his day, excavated the buildings from their sandy cocoon.

Despite having an unrivaled knowledge of ancient European societies, the indefatigable Childe had seen nothing like Skara Brae.[7] He uncovered eight well-preserved dwellings linked by low, covered passages. The walls of the houses still stand; the slab roofs of the passages were intact. Most important, the interior stone fittings of each dwelling survived. Each consisted of a large square room with a central fireplace, two beds on either side, and a dresser with shelves on the wall opposite the doorway. Thanks to radiocarbon dating we know that Skara Brae was occupied for six centuries between 3200 and 2200 BC, a settlement of Stone Age farmers. The history of beds in Britain entered the distant past for the first time.

The stone dwellings reflected a profound change in Orkney society. Until about three centuries earlier the Orcadians had dwelt in timber structures, whose interiors they divided into stalls. Intriguingly, this domestic design mirrored that of their tombs. It is hard to explain why they did this, but in their new world—in which they were now farming and investing in the land—perhaps they wanted to maintain clear links with their dead forebears. These were intimate settlements, probably organized around small kin-groups, where claims over the land must have been crucial and ancestral rights played a fundamental part of daily life.

Yet once they started making stone buildings, the equations of life and death appear to have changed significantly. Unlike wooden structures, the stone houses at Skara Brae and other contemporary settlements endured for generations. People now lived on in the solidly enduring homes of their forebears, sometimes possibly extending them, and again burying their ancestral dead close by. Farmers were now anchored to their fields and grazing grounds through many lifetimes. Both agriculture and building in stone required many people habitually working and living together.

In Hut 8 a shelved stone dresser faced the door. A hearth was in the center. Two stone bed boxes jutted from one wall, flanking the hearth on either side. The right-hand bed, as in all the houses, is larger than that on the left. Many have suggested that the larger bed was for men and the smaller for women, but some other division, perhaps age-related, could easily have been at work. In one of the houses higher phosphorus levels in a bed nearer the door tell us that bed-wetting babies and young children may have slept there. But this is speculation.

Larger beds were always to the right, smaller to the left. But unlike the Sibudu and Ohalo sleeping spaces, which appear to have had many uses, Skara Brae's beds were small and clearly meant for a more limited range of activities. They would have had space only for one adult and perhaps a child, especially once the box was lined with hides or furs. Although the restless sleeper might have felt cramped, in this chilly and windy climate warmth would have been more important. During the long, dark winters everyone would have spent much time wrapped in blankets and furs and lying or sitting by the hearth. This central, fire-lit zone would have been where people told stories, talked, joked, nursed, ate, and maybe, given their cramped beds and very different ideas about privacy,

A house at Skara Brae, Orkney Islands, Scotland, with putative stone bed
enclosures to right and left.

had sex too. At night they may have retreated to the cozy solitude
of their bed boxes. Holes around some of the boxes suggest that
beds were perhaps surrounded by rails holding curtains, either for
warmth or to keep out the summer light of the Scottish isles.

But nearby, in Hut 7, something else was going on. This house
was completely detached from its neighbors and could be reached
only by a side passage. Inside, the bodies of two women were found
lying in a stone-built grave under the right-hand bed and wall section. The women rested in a stone cist decorated with carvings that
was constructed before the structure was built. Perhaps their burial
was part of a foundation ritual—the door of Hut 7 could be secured
only from the outside, presumably to keep the occupants in. Archaeologists have puzzled over the meaning of Hut 7. Was this isolated structure a place where the dead were laid out in a bed before

burial? Or was it a birth house, separating the rituals surrounding childbirth from daily life? Or did these burials again reflect a concern for the continuity of life, between past, present, and future? In farming societies the endless cycle of winter, spring, summer, and autumn, of planting, growth, and harvest, defined human existence. The symbolism of birth, growth to adulthood, then death was a compelling reminder that life had been this way in the time of the ancestors and would remain the same in the lives of the unborn.

Yet the sleepers have long departed; the hides, textiles, or grass that gave them warmth and comfort have evaporated into a transitory past. How can we be sure we are even looking at beds? Even at the well-preserved Skara Brae site Childe had to make informed guesses. More recent discoveries tell us that he was almost certainly right. A contemporary village of some fifteen freestanding structures at Barnhouse, just north of the sacred circle known as the Stones of Stenness on Antaness Point on Orkney's main island, has stone furniture that includes more box beds. One house also had six recesses that may have served as beds.[8]

The Orcadian furniture has survived because it was stone built— but what happens when the beds were fashioned from wood, supported by stakes? Most of the time everything has vanished. Just occasionally, however, skilled excavation reveals a jigsaw of stake holes that stand out as discolorations in light soil. Beds, or at least their supports, appear miraculously before our eyes. At the other end of Britain, lying on white chalk subsoil, is the great earthen enclosure (or henge) of Durrington Walls, three kilometers northeast of Stonehenge. The archaeologist Mike Parker Pearson and his colleagues are consummate experts at interpreting the meanings of inconspicuous soil discolorations.[9] With brushes and trowels they identified the wooden stake holes of the hut walls and also shallow grooves in the chalk where horizontal planks or logs once lay. These were beam slots: all that remained of the foundations of bed boxes and storage bins. Parker Pearson thought immediately of the Skara Brae beds, but these boxes had been set in wood. There was more. One large, square house beside an avenue leading from Durrington Walls to the nearby river had an entrance facing south and a plaster floor. Along the west wall were the foundations of a box bed, with another one on the opposite wall. Another three houses also contained bed boxes set around central fireplaces. The beds of Durrington Walls are now but shadowy ghosts in chalky soil.

In the Durrington Walls and the Orcadian villages beds functioned as places to sleep and keep warm. But judging from the Orkney discoveries even these simple sleeping places had profound symbolic meanings as symbols of continuity. Contemporaneous beds found on the small, central Mediterranean islands of Gozo and Malta were similarly imbued with meaning and symbolism. Yet these beds also include a key innovation: legs.

Between 3500 and 2500 BC, just as civilizations were first developing in Egypt and Mesopotamia, small-scale farming societies on Malta and Gozo enjoyed a sophisticated art tradition centered on burial places and temples. The people lived in small farming communities linked by communal burial sites and ritual centers scattered across the two islands. These were isolated societies reachable only by hazardous voyages in simple watercraft. Their isolation seems to have given birth to an exceptionally rich vision of the cosmos centered on sacred places.

The ancient temples on Gozo and Malta were complex places. Narrow entrances led to an external forecourt where onlookers could watch unfolding rituals. Carefully designed lines of sight directed one's eyes from entrance corridors toward altars and places where ritual objects such as models and figurines were displayed. The temple interiors are comprised of oval rooms and corridors, but few people appear to have entered the inner precincts, which had bars across the passages. The ritual metaphors behind the compartments and the art elude us. Below-ground burial places, or hypogea, mirrored the temple format but were labyrinthine and of greater restricted access. In these places, where communities gathered for ritual observances related to burial of the dead, we find unexpected evidence of beds.

The richly painted walls of the hypogea show both male and female human figures seated or lying on a couch or bed.[10] Seven such bed figures are represented by sculptures, with several from burial sites, as if depicting death as a long sleep. All of them wear skirts, perhaps a mark of status. One sleeping woman, from the Hal Saflieni hypogeum on Malta, lies face down with her arms outstretched and her legs straight. Her head is propped on one arm, as if she were resting comfortably. The archaeologist Caroline Malone believes this posture may reflect a dreamlike experience, perhaps travel between layers of a layered cosmos, the realms of the living, the dead, and the supernatural. A pair of sculpted figures from Brochtorff on Gozo sits upright on a bed holding a small person, perhaps a child, and an offering cup. These are stately figures seated on a bed adorned with curvilinear patterns. They were placed near numerous small cups for red ocher. Malone speculates that these vessels as well as many nearby skeletons smothered in red ochre may reflect the timeless cycle of birth, living, and death. Two sculpted bed figures from a rubbish heap outside another site, Tarxien, on Malta, had torsos, or perhaps just heads, that could be moved. One of them has plump legs that extend over the side of the bed, while small figures below look out from between the bed struts. Perhaps these layered representations reflect ancestral deities that protected generations of the living and dead. The beds themselves had crossed struts and bindings turned into saucer-shaped, comfortable resting places with several layers of reeds or straw that were woven and tied to the frame. The beds seem to have had short, stubby legs.

The so-called sleeping woman of Hal Saflieni, Malta, c. 3000 BC.

The design of the temples and their underground burial places appears to reflect a vision of the living and supernatural worlds as a many-layered cosmos stretching from an underground world of death and into the heavens. Not all was placid in the ancient Maltese world, but many of the images, including the Hal Saflieni woman, reflect a calm and comfortable existence. Here, beds were far more than places for everyday activities. They were cosmological platforms linking the living with their ancestors.

SLEEPING LOW

Despite the early evidence of beds on legs, most people slept on the ground. Even today many people across the globe, especially subsistence farmers and the poor, have known nothing else. To sleep on a bed elevated off the ground set one apart and was an early sign of rank. If you were a commoner in pharaonic Egypt, you almost certainly slept on the floor, perhaps with a reed mat or even a crude mattress filled with straw or wool to cushion you from the hard surface. Challenging as it may sound to sleepers cushioned by modern mattress technology, it is said to be good for your body.

The physiotherapist Michael Tetley has a lifetime of experience studying nonhuman primates and people sleeping directly on the ground. When he commanded a platoon of African soldiers in 1953–54, they taught him how to sleep on his side on the ground but without a pillow so he could use both ears to listen for danger. He had found that mountain gorillas, chimpanzees, and gibbons sleep on their sides without any form of pillow. Many humans do the same, using an arm as a pillow and shifting their shoulders so that their neck is fully supported.

Tetley catalogued all manner of safe ways of sleeping without beds, some of them previously unrecorded. Tibetan nomads sleep on their shins, while Saharan peoples sometimes sleep squatting. For those accustomed to these positions, they are apparently perfectly comfortable.[11] Not a man to shy away from practicalities, Tetley even recorded the various positions outdoor ground-sleeping males can adopt in order to avoid having their penises bitten by bugs. However, few humans opt to sleep naked prone on the open ground: we feel too vulnerable, not least to the creeping insects, imagined or otherwise, that might bite or burrow into our skin or various orifices.

For some populations ground sleeping was preferred over beds: a deliberate cultural and aesthetic choice, regardless of wealth or status. In Asia sleeping on the floor was routine even after the raised platform as bed appeared in China as early as the thirteenth to eleventh centuries BC. The Japanese habitually slept on the floor until modern times. From perhaps the eighth century AD they used throw mats, or straw mats shaped roughly to the human body, that covered the entire floor of a room, known as *tatami* (from the verb *tatamu*, to fold). Tatami were used for both bedding and seating and became so standardized that they were used to compile housing statistics: the number of tatami coincided with the number of rooms in a house. The *futon*, a cotton mattress stuffed with batting and placed on a mat-covered floor, came into use during the seventeenth century. Futons have the huge advantage of being portable. In today's crowded urban apartments they can be folded away, allowing the sleeping space to be used for other purposes.

Elevated beds were unknown in the Ottoman court at Constantinople. Even the sultan slept on a low platform covered with rugs and cushions, the bed being nothing more than a slightly raised portion of the floor. You could sleep wherever you could lay down bedding. Religious mendicants often favored the floor in the belief that sleeping on a hard surface connected them to the spiritual virtues of poverty. However, once you start using a bed and elevate yourself off the ground, the dynamics of sleep change, pillows often become necessary, and you become much more susceptible to lower back pain. Sleeping on the ground or some other hard surface was therefore not necessarily a bad thing until issues of social prestige came into play. Beds with legs were almost always a way of symbolizing social elevation, generally for the affluent or the nobility.

SLEEPING HIGH

Given that social inequality is a hallmark of civilization, it is no surprise that its emergence brings elevated beds on legs into sharper focus. The Sumerians of Mesopotamia used wooden bed frames on legs. Early Egyptian beds were little more than wooden frames with legs, as leather or cloth strips or carefully woven reeds formed the sleeping platform. Many of these raised beds had legs of unequal length, the tallest end being at the head. A footrest sometimes formed the lower end.

Arid climates are the bed excavator's best friend, for wooden objects often survive the millennia. The desert air of Egypt has preserved some imposing beds. The Vizier Mereruka lived at the end of the VI Dynasty (c. 2300 BC) and served King Teti. As the second most important person in Egypt after the ruler he had heavy responsibilities, among them "Overseer of the Royal Record Scribes."[12] Mereruka married Teti's daughter Sesheshet Watetkhethor, making him the pharaoh's son-in-law. At their death the couple was buried in a thirty-three-room chapel at Saqqara in Lower Egypt. The paintings and engravings on the sepulcher walls have left us a colorful impression of their daily activities—and of their bed.

Five chambers of the chapel belong to his wife, Watetkhethor. In one scene the vizier sits at the head of the marital bed, his elbow apparently resting on a headrest, while Watetkhethor kneels at the foot playing a harp. Offering and storage jars as well as boxes are stowed neatly underneath. Another register in the tomb shows a large bed with lion's feet. Two men are spreading the linen as five attendants wait and watch with their hands crossed, all of them bearing the title "overseer of linen." Mereruka approaches the bed, holding his wife's hand, followed by male and female attendants. In the next panel the sheets are in place and the headrest is in position. The painting symbolizes the couple's impending sexual union. Mereruka is called "He of the made bed," while Watetkhethor was "She of the headrest." This scene is as erotic as ancient Egyptian artists got when painting on tomb walls. Birth and rebirth surrounded noble and royal beds. Headrests, made of stone, clay, or wood, were associated with the rising sun and with rebirth and served the living as well as the dead.

As the pharaoh's son-in-law, Mereruka owned a bed of the highest quality. Three centuries earlier, in about 2580 to 2575 BC, Queen Hetepheres went to eternity with magnificent furniture that included a canopied bed on legs sheathed in gold. The wood having

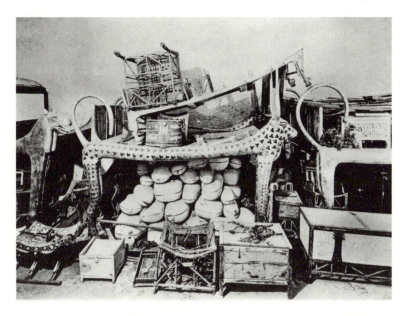

Tutankhamun's funerary beds in the antechamber of his tomb, 1922.

long since rotted away, the Egyptologist George Reisner reconstructed the bed by assembling the collapsed metal sheets. Many centuries later the boy-king Tutankhamun went to eternity with six feline-footed beds, the most spectacular fashioned from ebony and covered with thick gold leaf.[13] The gold leaf bears scratches, as if the bed had been used. Three prefabricated funerary beds lay in the antechamber of his tomb, their higher ends decorated with animal-headed figures. One bed featured lions' heads and represented the "lion-bed" used to mummify the corpse. Another was adorned with hippopotamus heads and was probably devoted to the Taweret, the goddess of childbirth and fertility. A bed with a cow's head may have further evoked the cow goddess Mehetweret, again linked to powerful ideas of rebirth and creation.

Strong symbolism surrounded every deed of the pharaoh, including his sex life. Every minute aspect of his daily routine was regimented and organized. As the Greek historian Diodorus Siculus wrote of a pharaoh in the first century BC, "There was a set time not only for his holding audiences and rendering judgments, but even for his taking a walk, bathing, and sleeping with his wife, and in a word for every act of his life."[14] The same may have been true centuries earlier for senior officials like Mereruka, whose tomb wall suggests that duty followed him even as he approached his bed in the company of his wife.

Later in ancient times beds were the subject of abiding myths. Greek and Roman literature abounds with references to their ability to comfort and provide refuge. The beds of the wealthy in both Greece and Rome resembled those of the Egyptians—narrow rectangles in their most basic form—but they had higher legs and often doubled as tables. There were no footboards, but headboards were provided for leaning against while reclining. The well-known Greek *kliné* originated as a dining couch but soon became a common deathbed. Interlaced flax or leather straps supported the mattress. Inevitably a diverse Roman vocabulary elaborated on the generic Latin word *lectus* ("bed") and reflected its many uses. People slept on *lectus cubicularis*, a bed associated with a bedroom, *cubiculum* being a bedroom, or on *lectus genialis*, the marriage bed, for more amorous nights. The *lectus discubitorius* was a table bed for eating, generally on one's left side to leave the right hand free. There were usually three people to such a bed, the most important guest in the middle. There were *lecti* for studying and working, beds on wheels for the sick, and beds that held tightly bound lunatics. *Lectus funebris* carried the dead to the funeral pyre.[15]

Beds were platforms for rich Chinese as well. Gu Kaizhi (c. AD 345–406) was the father of Chinese classical painting. His master handscroll painting in nine scenes *The Admonitions of the Instructress to the Court Ladies* shows an emperor and his concubine eyeing one another suspiciously—careless words can foster distrust. They sit on a bed platform with four posts that support a fine fabric canopy. This provided a degree of separation in royal palaces where there were no discrete sleeping rooms.

The beds may have been hard, a common preference in China today, but the rich and powerful liked their beds to be surrounded by fine sheets. The Chinese expertise with textiles produced lavish bed hangings, often embroidered with auspicious symbols such as flying mythic figures. In time the headrest gave way to pillows. These had the advantage of allowing users to recline at an angle and engage in social activities other than sleeping while keeping their elaborate hairdo intact.

The basic designs of beds changed little over the millennia. In most places the closer to the floor you slept, the poorer you were. The noble and wealthy slept on raised beds, swathed in comfortable fabrics. Being raised above the ground, your bed surrounded by hangings, perhaps to ward off mosquitoes or cold drafts, was a sign of social status. The poor had to be content with the floor. Wealthier Greeks and especially Romans slept on narrow beds with a sloped surface, higher at the head, fashioned by bolsters, just as pharaohs had done thousands of years earlier.

EUROPEAN FASHIONS

The distinction between noble, wealthy, and commoner persisted into medieval Europe. Peasants, that is, most people, would literally hit the hay, perhaps wrapped in a simple blanket or a cloak. Early modern beds came in forms ranging from simple straw piles on an earthen floor or straw-filled sacks on raised platforms to box beds set into walls and truckle beds on wheels. In the twelfth century beds grew wider, sometimes up to four meters wide, and gradually became more solid pieces of furniture, high enough off the ground that things could be stored beneath. Atop lay an under mattress filled with straw, then an upper mattress of linen or wool, followed by a feather mattress covered with a bedsheet.

The basic elements of the modern bed were in place by late medieval times. Surviving bedding of the era's superrich includes such splendors as the Tristan Quilt, now in London's Victoria and Albert Museum. Made of linen and padded with cotton wadding, it was created in Sicily around 1360–1400 and embroidered with a version of the then-popular legend of Tristan and Isolde in no fewer than fourteen scenes. The museum's index card tells us that it "must have looked particularly impressive by candlelight, with lively scenes of battles, ships and castles."[16] Quite so, but to the modern eye, it also looks heavy and rough.

In addition to the quilts and covers blanketing the bed, the medieval European sleeper's head might lie on a raised bolster extended across the bed, while cushions and pillows enabled sitting up in comfort and probably sleeping partially seated too. Why they slept at an angle, sometimes almost upright, is unclear. It may have been connected to the propensity for mattresses to sag, or to a fear of lying flat—a posture widely associated with death. The seventeenth-century Dutch artist Rembrandt van Rijn may have slept almost vertically in one of the cramped box beds in his Amsterdam house. Some men regarded pillows as effeminate, and a surprising number chose to rest their heads on logs. Although sleeping on wood sounds unappealing, hard headrests were not new: early Chinese, Ancient Egyptian, Nubian, Greek, and, later, Japanese and African headrests were often made of rigid materials, with a dip to cradle the hair.

High-society beds in medieval Europe aimed to impress and were often surrounded by canopies that hung directly from the ceiling. In an era when fresh air was considered unhealthy, the curtains kept in the warmth while offering the added benefit of keeping out the night's devils, witches, and ghosts. Around 1290 John Fontin, a well-off merchant, commissioned just such a canopied bed for his house in Southampton, England. Today, you can see a reconstructed version of it tucked away in the corner of a room replete with heavy drapes. Toward the end of the fifteenth century the Italians came up with a new solution to protect against chills and devils: the four-poster bed with curtains hanging directly from an attached frame.

These beds soon became de rigueur among the rich in Tudor England. The four-poster bed came into wider use in more affluent European houses during the sixteenth to eighteenth centuries. Like many earlier models, they often had rope and canvas underpinnings and frames, which meant they came to resemble hammocks, even when the ropes were periodically tightened, and sleepers generally slipped to the middle. It is often claimed, particularly by guides in English stately homes, that this rope-tightening issue lies behind the old bedtime chant "Night night, sleep tight." This remains to be seen given that the phrase became widely used only in the twentieth century, the oldest known reference to it appearing in 1860.

Regardless of the saying's pedigree, rope tightening was certainly once the order of the day. Again, few people slept fully reclined in such beds but instead adopted half-seated sleeping positions. For the next two hundred years the wealthy competed with one another in making the four-posters more beautiful as well as bigger, until at times they almost filled whole rooms. In premodern European times beds were often the most desirable and expensive item of household furniture. They were major investments. To own a spare bed was a great luxury. As the seventeenth-century London diarist Samuel Pepys wrote, "Mighty proud I am that I am able to have a spare bed for my friends."[17]

Life was more restrained in the American colonies. Most of the earliest colonists' beds mirrored what the people had left behind: Dutch or English in style, with thick, pile bedcovers to keep out the cold and wet. Those from the Netherlands favored the cupboard, or box bed, ubiquitous in their homeland in the seventeenth century. They were usually not stand-alone furniture but built directly into the room's wall paneling.

With the nineteenth century, modernization and sanitation were increasingly the Western order of the day. The English textile designer William Morris designed clean, attractive bed hangings with fabrics made of lightweight cotton rather than heavy wools, damasks, or fragile silk.[18] Morris still loved his old bed, though, and usually slept in his family's seventeenth-century four-poster—though he surrounded it with new curtains designed by his daughter. A poem he composed runs around the valance and ends with the line, "Right good is rest."

Right good rest was particularly needed now that people had to work longer and longer hours outside the home. With industrialization, many households threw away the old mattresses that tended to be stuffed with whatever was available—wool, moss, rags. Factory-made iron bedstead with metal springs came into fashion. Such beds would ideally have a tough horsehair mattress, a feather mattress, various layers of bottom and top sheets, three or four blankets, an eiderdown, pillows, and pillow cases. For the middle and upper classes, household standards could be high, some housekeeping manuals advocating the daily turning of the mattress and twice-daily changing of pillow cases. Servants were a must.

Only after the devastation of the First World War did the old hierarchical system of staff and servants begin to disappear in the West. Once maids were in short supply, making up a convoluted bed became a loathsome chore. Trendy households sighed a sigh of relief in the 1970s when the Swedish duvet was popularized by the designer Terence Conran. For the first time ever, the bed on legs could be made in three seconds flat. Not only can our beds now be easily made up, they can also be cheaply bought from global factories. Despite being our most-used piece of furniture, beds now garner no comment and are hidden away.[19] Yet our beds reveal who we are, how we live, and what we think—and always have.

TWO

Sleep through Time

In his 1612 manual "Approved Directions for Health" the Welsh writer William Vaughan wrote that sleep "strengtheneth all the spirits, comforteth the body, quieteth the humours . . . taketh away sorrow, and asswageth furie of the mind."[1] An Italian saying of the day added, "Bed is a medicine," echoing established medical opinion that sleep was critical to health. For some, sleep was a way "to forget the world," according to an East Anglian saying. Many believed that sleep even shaped one's fortune on both sides of the grave. The pessimistic William Phiston (or Fiston), in his book *Schoole of Good Manners* (1609), described the dark night as a symbol of "horror, dark, and woe." He called his bed a prototype for his grave.[2]

In a world in which countless people were terrified of the dark, a good night's sleep was a guardian of the soul's health, and the bed in which one slept was a place of physical and spiritual transformation. During the nineteenth century Victorians surrounded themselves with familiar objects, gazed at religious images embroidered on their bedding, prayed, and read from the scriptures before sleeping. You made your peace with God, ideally on bended knee, every night before slumber. Spiritual fears of sleep have receded in the face of the secular in our busy world. Today, most think of sleep simply as a thing for eliminating tiredness. While our dreams, if we can remember them, are usually something best kept to ourselves.

The ancient Egyptians set great store by dreams, believing they allowed gods to deliver guiding messages. The best way to induce or "incubate" such visions was to visit a sanctuary or shrine and sleep overnight with a special "dream." Some of these books used to interpret dreams still exist. The one compiled around 1275 BC by the scribe Qenhirkopeshef from Deir el-Medina, the home of the workmen who built the tombs in the Valley of the Kings, offered interpretations of over a hundred dreams, which the author categorized as either auspicious or inauspicious. Auspicious dreams included: "If a man sees himself burying an old man, it is good, meaning prosperity." Among the inauspicious: "If a man sees himself in a dream making love to a woman, it is bad, because it means mourning." The Egyptians almost always regarded sexual dreams as bad, especially for women—even dreaming of sex with her husband was a bad omen. The few positive female sexual dreams tend to involve animals, such as this cheerily domestic one from the Papyrus Carlsberg XIII: "If an ibis has intercourse with her, she [will] have a well-equipped house."[3] Scribes used the word *ad* (a bed on legs) to denote sleep, adding the word *rswt* (shown by an open eye) to express the dream. The literal translation of *rswt* is "to come awake." Thus the hieroglyph for a dream is the symbol of bed combined with that of an open eye. This symbol encapsulates the Egyptian view of dreams: as an awakened state within sleep—a way to communicate with the gods and the afterworld and a way to heal and guide one's life.

Sleep temples continued under the Greeks. Like the Egyptians, most Greeks believed the gods sent dreams as messages or guidance.

In his work *On Divination in Sleep* a pragmatic Aristotle questioned this notion, concluding that dreams were more likely simply images based on past experiences and thoughts. Nonetheless, belief in the prophetic potential of dreams remained strong: Jesus dreamt of his betrayal. The Roman emperor Caligula dreamt he stood before the throne of Jupiter—king of all the gods—before being kicked down to earth, a vision he thought to be a premonition of his death. He was assassinated the next day.

In 1590 the young Lucrecia de León of Madrid was arrested because the Spanish authorities said her dreams were causing "scandal and unrest." As recorded over a period of years by a couple of priests, Lucrecia's roughly four thousand apocalyptic visions had included Spain's defeat by English and Turkish troops and the end of the world. Only one important dream came true: the wreck of the Armada. Even her own father told her that "dreams are only dreams" and "if you believe in them I will give the order to have you killed." Ultimately, she was sentenced to receive one hundred lashes and serve two years in a convent.

Some dreams were divine on other levels, if problematic to marital harmony. At the height of the 1666 London plague the diarist Samuel Pepys recorded an imagined night of passion with Lady Castlemaine as "the best that ever was dreamed." His wife, Elisabeth de St Michel, was so suspicious that she took to checking the sleeping Pepys's penis for signs of an erection. Then again, their marriage was troubled enough by his real-life infidelities, including with Deb Willet, a woman employed to help Elisabeth. Though when Elisabeth died of typhoid, at the age of just twenty-nine, it was said to have affected the thirty-six-year-old Pepys so severely that he never again kept his diary.

Dream recording reached dizzying heights among the upper classes of eighteenth-century England. One London tradesman grew rich on his Nocturnal Remembrancer, a tablet of parchment with a horizontal guide for recording dreams by candlelight.[4] With the nineteenth century, a new group of thinkers returned to the life-guiding importance of dreams. The leader of them all was Sigmund Freud. In *The Interpretation of Dreams*, published in 1900, he argued that dreams are symbolic manifestations of repressed desires, fears, and wishes that are often too painful to experience or remember directly and so are sublimated into our subconscious through "psychic censorship."[5] In his analyses he returned to the work of the diviner Artemidorus of Ephesus, who translated numerous Egyptian dream symbols during the second century AD, such as that the right hand represented the father, son, or friend, and the left (sinister), the mother, wife, or mistress. Carl Jung also famously believed that dreams revealed secrets of the inner life and showed the dreamer hidden aspects of his or her personality. Their contemporary Alfred Adler preferred to see them as problem-solving devices, further suggesting that the more dreams you have (or remember), the more problems you tend to have.

The modern sleep researcher Jim Horne cautions that dreams are nothing more than B movies that deserve to be forgotten: "a surreal pastiche of what we have recently encountered and thought about during wakefulness."[6] Some scientists speculate that the dreaming phases of sleep optimize physical and mental recuperation as well as some aspects of memory consolidation. Nonetheless, the age-old importance of dreams is hard for some to shake. Kelly Bulkeley, a psychologist of religion, director of the Sleep and Dream Database, and the brains behind such dream analysis sites as the Donald Trump–focused "IDreamOfTrump.net," thinks dreams are crucial to understanding life.

Occasionally dreams seem to contain awakened inspiration, as the ancient Egyptians might have said. The French philosopher Descartes claimed that a series of dreams he experienced one night in 1619 revealed to him the basis of the new scientific method (although we must also recognize the Arab polymath Ibn al-Haythan, who formulated the scientific method five centuries earlier). James Watson, the codiscoverer of the structure of DNA, dreamt of a spiral staircase, the clue to the double helix—though this may have happened after he had seen the structure revealed in Rosalind Franklin's X-ray diffraction images. Mary Shelley said *Frankenstein* was inspired by a dream. A depressed Hergé dreamed of Tintin in Tibet. Paul McCartney dreamed up the melody of "Yesterday," initially assuming it was simply an old song remembered from his childhood, and *The Terminator* came to James Cameron while he was ill with a fever.

A huge literature surrounds dreams in many non-Western societies. Australian Aborigines prefer to sleep close to fellow kin, for how one sleeps influences one's spirit's ability to connect with the Dreaming.[7] Individuals with supernatural power claim they can access powerful metaphysical realms and travel to places out of reach to ordinary folk. They acquire such powers by sleeping in significant locations or from spirits that visit them during sleep. Sleep deprivation is a method of spiritual revelation and empowerment among Native American groups, a condition in which people on solitary vision quests enter trancelike states to travel. A shaman could close his eyes and travel enormous distances with his mind, leaving his body behind. These journeys remain with the practitioner, part of a matrix of cultural knowledge, personal experience, and relationships that fuse into experiences that defy natural law. Dream visions exercise a potent, if often inconspicuous, influence on many non-Western societies.

TICKTOCK

Dreaming is, of course, part of a far longer sleep process. All living beings operate a daily internal biological clock, or circadian rhythm. In humans, twenty thousand nonseeing nerve cells behind the eye register environmental cues, including the presence of light, to keep our body clock's time.

In the early 1990s Thomas Wehr, a psychiatrist at the US National Institute of Mental Health, placed a group of volunteers for a month in an environment that was dark for fourteen hours a day, in an attempt to replicate the natural world.[8] By the fourth week his group had settled into an average of eight hours' sleep—but not in one stretch. Instead, the volunteers tended to lie awake for one or two hours in the evening and then fall asleep quickly following a spike in the hormone melatonin, triggered by darkness. After three to five hours of sleep the subjects would awaken for an hour or two before falling asleep again for another three to five hours. Wehr described the intervening period as one of "non-anxious wakefulness," an almost "meditative state" that had its own endocrinology, including heightened levels of prolactin, the stress-reducing hormone associated with lactating mothers and orgasms. To Wehr, the experiment suggested that this biphasic pattern of sleep is the natural nocturnal rhythm for humans.

A historian at Virginia Tech, A. Roger Ekirch, was struck by Wehr's study and began collecting historical references to biphasic sleep.[9] Latin texts like Livy's *History of Rome* and Virgil's *Aeneid*, both written during the first century BC, contain multiple references to *primo somno* or *concubine nocte*, the first sleep. In medieval times, texts by authors including Chaucer reveal that Britons often went to bed for their "fyrste sleep" in the early evening, after which they would awaken, perhaps have something to eat, and then enjoy a second or morning sleep that might not begin until the small hours. During the night-waking period, which English speakers seem to have called the watch or watching, people might reflect on dreams, talk, smoke, eat, or have sex (Jewish texts advise that these hours are good for procreation). Others devoted their watches to pious ends.

Many religions regard the early morning hours as a particularly spiritual time. For example, the Quran advocates the performance of night prayers (the Tahajjud) at around 2:00 or 3:00 a.m., either at home or in the mosque. After praying, the faithful generally return to their beds, until arising again for the compulsory morning Fajr prayer. As early as the sixth century Saint Benedict of Nursia, the founder of the Benedictine order, required his monks to rise after midnight and recite psalms. By the High Middle Ages it was common for Catholics to pray in the quiet hours of the morning. These devotions had the added benefit of combating the devil. In Western folklore, witchcraft and black magic were said to be most effective in the early hours. From 1484 to 1750 around two hundred thousand Western European women were murdered for being witches: one of their crimes was being outside in the deep night for no good reason. The so-called witching hour, a phrase first recorded in 1883, embraced various night hours ranging from midnight to 4:00 a.m. Clearly it was an attempt to control women's movements.There is far more evidence that men used the watch to perform dark deeds. In 1680 the Reverend Anthony Horneck regretted how highwaymen and thieves rose at midnight to rob and murder people. A century later, in 1775, the Reverend J. Clayton published his humorless "Friendly Advice to the Poor," in which he warned of "the Danger of Midnight revels."

For others, particularly anonymous urban dwellers, work called. The early seventeenth-century composer Orlando Gibbons wrote the lyrics for a street-chanting market song entitled "The Cries of London." A single market trader opens with "God give you good morrow, my masters, past three o'clock and a fair morning." He is soon joined by a chorus of voices telling of all the goods on sale, the assumption being that people are available to buy them. The city was alive at three o'clock in the morning.

If segmented sleep was once so common, why have we forgotten about it, and why aren't there more references to it? Perhaps biphasic sleep was so normal that contemporaries felt little need to analyze it. Great seventeenth-century writers like George Wither and John Locke refer to it as a normal feature of life. Wrote Locke in 1690, "All men sleep by intervals," with no further comment. Moreover, the late seventeenth century saw a large increase in the number of people leaving diaries and other accounts that might refer to their sleeping patterns. Diaries from earlier times are much rarer. By then, however, artificial light and late hours had become fashionable among the wealthy—the most common writers of the texts. One conclusion, then, is that segmented sleep is specifically linked to a world without artificial light, which blurred the barrier between day and night.

Can anthropological research illuminate the debate? Twentieth-century studies of the nonindustrial and nonlamplight Tiv, Chagga, and G/wi farmers of Africa showed that biphasic sleeping was commonplace among all three groups.[10] As late as 1969 the Tiv subsistence farmers of central Nigeria used "first sleep" and "second sleep" as traditional intervals of time. On the other hand, a team led by Jerome Siegel of the UCLA Sleep Disorders Center studied three widely separated hunter-gatherer societies in Tanzania, Namibia, and Bolivia. In each case, the researchers found little evidence of segmented sleep at night but some evidence of daytime napping, especially during the summer months. They also found that people slept, on average, about six hours a night, less than the eight or nine hours often recommended by modern Western physicians. Yet none had the adverse health effects, such as obesity, diabetes, or mood disorders, that scientists often link to sleep deprivation. To Siegel's team, a straight sleep of about six hours seems to express "core human sleep patterns, most likely characteristic of pre-modern era *Homo sapiens.*"[11]

No modern human group, no matter how isolated, is an unchanged portal into the past. None of the groups being studied lives in pristine prehistoric isolation from the industrial world. The pioneers of anthropology, who did sometimes study groups that had never encountered westerners or modern technology, never mentioned sleep except for occasional references to who slept with whom and when. Beyond that, they considered it too mundane to be worth noting. The Polish-born anthropologist Bronislaw Malinowski (1884–1942), who spent long periods among the Trobriand Islanders of the southwestern Pacific, remarks frequently in his diaries that he "went to sleep." Yet he did so while the islanders were still wide awake and talking, a classic case of the different perspective on sleep between many anthropologists and their subjects. Though Malinowski dutifully described the huts in which they slept, he said almost nothing about beds or sleeping practices. He did note that sleep was a time of danger when raids could occur and when people were especially vulnerable to sorcery. Other early anthropologists, such as Alfred Radcliffe-Brown (1881–1955), who studied the Nuer pastoralists of the Nile, made similar observations.

Ultimately, every society teaches its young about sleeping in different ways, for sleep is both a biological and a cultural phenomenon. Moreover, *Homo sapiens* are great adaptors. We have always had many ways of doing things, and we cannot assume that all humans have always slept the same way. While biphasic sleep seems to be the dominant model in the few anthropological studies on sleep in nonindustrial societies, it is most likely not the only way we ever slept. Still, our tendency toward biphasic sleep patterns may explain some of our modern bedtime troubles.

INDUSTRIALIZING SLEEP

In our modern world, governed by schedules, an entire industry has arisen to help us sleep and wake on cue. The first modern sleeping pill was developed in 1903, a synthetic barbiturate called Veronal. By 1930 the number of barbiturates taken annually in the United States topped one billion doses. In 2013 a Centers for

Disease Control report stated that nine million Americans, or 4 percent of all US adults, use prescription sleeping pills. Worldwide spending on sleep aids was estimated to be about $58 billion in 2014, a figure projected to rise to over $100 billion by 2023. The bitter truth is that these pills tend to increase sleep by just twenty minutes and are laden with side effects, ranging from increased risks of falls to dementia.

Yet sleep remedies are nothing new. The Roman emperor Publius Licinius Valerianus (AD 253–60) was such a champion of a concoction made from the herb valerian that it was named after him. Opium was another long-running favorite. Ancient Egyptian medical papyri recommended mixing it with lavender and chamomile. In the sixteenth century a French physician suggested inserting a grain of opium behind the ear, in a hole to be made by a blood-sucking leech. Most wealthy sixteenth-century insomniacs preferred the easier option of drinking laudanum, a combination of opium and diluted alcohol. In nineteenth-century Europe and the United States the leading sleep potion was a blend of alcohol, sugar, and opium known as wine (or tincture) of opium, a morphine-like mix that was often cheaper than a shot of gin or wine. Alcohol by itself was a remedy too: many Germans sipped a boozy *Schlaftrincke* ("sleep drink") before bed.

The exponential boom in sleep aids has gone hand in hand with the Industrial Revolution. Human evolutionists might see such pills as yet another human adaptation: we need them because industrial capitalism has put us on a strict timetable. Most of us have to get up in time for work, which is usually outside the home, and we need to work the correct hours. In the words of the journalist Arianna Huffington, with industrialization, sleep "became just another commodity to be exploited as much as possible."[12] This cultural indoctrination starts young: five-year-old children are forced to get up for school on schedule and are penalized if late. Thomas

Jefferson, hardly a staunch advocate of industrialization, saw universal schooling as a key requisite of a democratic republic—but as practiced, it also conveniently readies the next generation for the relentless timetabled expectations of the workplace.

This inculcation means that if we awaken in the small hours, perhaps adhering to our natural biphasic sleep pattern, we may be gripped by fear: how will we manage the coming day? Billions of us take a pill, others just fret. Yet before the age of pocket watches, factory rosters, and train timetables, sleep had no schedule. The only consequence was that the later the bedtime, the later the watch and the later the second sleep. For instance, in Chaucer's "The Squire's Tale" the King of Tartary's daughter Canacee sleeps "soon after evening fell" and then wakes in early morning following her first sleep, whereas her fellow travelers stay up much later and then sleep until daylight.

The industrial era added a new temptation: the night suddenly became a lamplit playground. Not that the idea was new. Street lighting of a kind illuminated parts of Roman Ephesus and Antioch. Islamic Córdoba in southern Spain had some lighting in the ninth century AD. But such lights were far from universal until the Industrial Revolution. The proliferation of cheap gas and electric light meant that by the late nineteenth century it was no longer only the aristocracy who could stay up late. Matthew Walker, a sleep researcher at the University of California, Berkeley, argues that the resultant resistance to sleep is making us fat, ill, and depressed.[13]

In the past, night was a dark time. Some of our work as archaeologists has taken us to exceedingly remote regions, where we could experience a flavor of the electricity-free world. When we were excavating a site on an isolated patch of Yemen's Red Sea plain, a typical evening would go something like this: sit around the campfire until after dark (which in winter could be early), realize how utterly dark it was, turn on flashlight, attract apocalyptic clog of winged insects, turn off flashlight, remember we had to get up with the sun at 5:00 a.m., retreat to safety of tents to sleep. The oppression of the night is sometimes forgotten in our modern world. In English, the darkness used to have its own name: night season. Even in large European towns medieval travelers hired lantern-bearers to help them navigate the road. In London they were called link boys, and they would carry a flaming torch to light the way and act as an escort.[14]

Things began to change only in 1667, under Louis XIV of France. His royal government began installing oil lanterns on the Paris streets, putting three thousand in place by 1670 and double that number by 1730. By the end of the seventeenth century over fifty cities across Europe had followed the Paris example. In 1807 Pall Mall in London became the first city street to be illuminated by lamps that burned coal gas. By 1823 nearly forty thousand lamps lit over two hundred miles of London's streets.

Public lighting revolutionized city life. Well-lit streets helped protect people who were once prey for lurking robbers as they walked out in the dark. For the first time, all classes of rapidly growing urban societies could enjoy a nightlife and socialize until the small hours. Boisterous evening revelers brought their own issues, late night pubs and bars being a particular focus of public outrage. For this and many other reasons, in the first half of the nineteenth century London introduced its first professional police service. Gradually, bedtime became safer and better protected. Despite all of our modern sleep woes a feeling of safety is conducive to sleep—which is why sleep researchers have found that pet cats and domesticated horses sleep longer when they are protected in houses or pens.[15] Perhaps some of our modern sleep losses are balanced by forgotten gains.

What of the notion that sleep avoidance actually improves productivity? Many of our leaders claim to need little sleep—among them Margaret Thatcher, Bill Clinton, and Donald Trump. Again, to quote Arianna Huffington, "Going without sleep became . . . a sign of strength, the way of measuring masculinity, maximum efficiency." Yet this masculinity is not an exclusively modern trait, as every single one of the world's civilizations (or every one that has left written records) has been patriarchal: the men rule. Machismo goes back to ancient Mesopotamia.

Some of history's greatest generals were admired as short-sleepers, among them Alexander, Hannibal, and Napoleon. Winston Churchill, perhaps the best-known short-sleeping leader, believed in the midday nap, which some scientists have since identified as part of our inbuilt circadian rhythm. "You must sleep sometimes between lunch and dinner, and no half-way measures," he advised. "Take off your clothes and go to bed. That's what I always do. Don't think you will be doing less work because you sleep during the day. . . . You will be able to accomplish more. You get two days in one. . . . When the war started, I had to sleep during the day because that was the only way I could cope with my responsibilities."[16] This habit is what allowed him to go to bed very late in the evening and sleep for just four hours, to the distress of his staff. Churchill not only slept in his bed but also made momentous decisions, interviewed generals and ministers, and plotted the defeat of Adolf Hitler there.

Other dynamic people have professed to be short-sleepers. Leonardo da Vinci is, perhaps apocryphally, said to have created the *Mona Lisa* on two hours of sleep a day, broken up into a fifteen-minute nap every four hours. Benjamin Franklin coined the killjoy phrase "Early to bed, early to rise makes a man healthy, wealthy, and wise"—yet his diaries show that he actually got quite a lot of sleep, usually from 10:00 p.m. to 5:00 a.m. Voltaire took four hours a night, though this regime was undoubtedly facilitated by his habit of drinking forty cups of coffee a day. It is no coincidence that coffee consumption has grown massively with the industrial era.

Most people suffer if they don't get enough sleep: short-sleeper Winston Churchill, for instance, is well known for the "black dog" of depression that haunted him. Yet there is a rare group of people who, with no effort, average only around five hours per night with no adverse health effects. Known as natural short-sleepers, this elite group tends to be positive and optimistic in outlook. Very long sleep, by contrast, is linked with low mood. Thomas Edison, who did more than anyone else to end the practice of biphasic sleep, was among history's natural short-sleepers. He is said to have needed only around four hours a night, which he often took in a cot in his office or on the floor near his work table. Disdainful of those who thought they needed more, at the age of eighty he wrote in the *New York Times*, "The future man will spend less time in bed. . . . In the old days man went up and down with the sun. . . . A million years from now he won't go to bed at all. Really, sleep is an absurdity, a bad habit. . . . Nothing in this world is more dangerous to the efficiency of humanity than too much sleep."[17]

Predictably in our clock-driven age, early waking is trumpeted as the key to fame and riches. When the Young Men's Early Rising Association was founded in 1859, its members said their success was due to early mornings. Their ideology is echoed in the Miracle Morning, an online movement led by the ebullient DJ and author Hal Elrod, who urges his followers to get up at 5:00 a.m. to enjoy phenomenal productivity. In the interest of research, we both tried it: it worked. We had never been so productive—for about a week. But then we got tired, we missed our evening revelries, and our beds called. We are now disciples of Tom Hodgkinson, editor of *The Idler* magazine and several books on idling, whose philosophy extols staying in bed longer and enjoying life more.

But how much longer should we be staying in our beds? In 2002 Dan Kripke of the Scripps Sleep Center led a huge study involving over a million North Americans to determine optimum amounts of sleep. He reported that death rates were lowest in people sleeping around seven hours per day (then the average for the United States).[18] By 2017 the Sleep Council's "Great British Bedtime Report" revealed that 74 percent of Brits get fewer than seven hours' sleep, 12 percent get under five, and 30 percent report getting "a poor sleep most nights." The solution to all this is elusive, but we wish everyone could find a way to get preindustrial: to work for ourselves and keep our own bedtimes. Those who found their natural sleep pattern was biphasic would simply wake in the night and do as they wished—rather than reach for the sleeping pills or panicking at every tock of the alarm clock. After all, much can be done in bed.

THREE

The Big Bang

In AD 64 the Roman emperor Nero married his fifth spouse. Nero took the role of blushing bride, and his husband was the freedman Pythagoras or possibly Doryphorus—the ancient sources don't agree. What's certain is that this was a scandalous wedding. An outraged Tacitus wrote, "Nero, who polluted himself by every lawful or lawless indulgence, had not omitted a single abomination which could heighten his depravity, till a few days afterwards he stooped to marry himself to one of that filthy herd, by name Pythagoras, with all the forms of regular wedlock. The bridal veil was put over the emperor; people saw the witnesses of the ceremony, the wedding dower, the couch [bed] and the nuptial torches."[1]

In Roman times the function of marriage was to continue the male line through the production of children, preferably boys, who would go on to serve in the army or in the administrations of overseas territories. For prominent families in the Greek and Roman societies, as in many others, one's children were also pawns in high-powered political games. Sex with one's spouse was an expected duty, as was serial childbirth for women. The virility of husband and wife ensured survival of the hereditary line, and the entire empire depended on procreation. Musonius Rufus, who taught Stoic philosophy until Nero exiled him, argued that the only reason for having genitals and getting married was to have children—to ensure humanity's survival.[2]

Our sexuality has presumably changed little since the first *Homo sapiens* emerged over three hundred thousand years ago. Despite individual variations, we experience the same sex drives as Palaeolithic artists, Egyptian pharaohs, or Victorian ladies. But the way we have dealt with this drive has ranged from the austere to the decadent and everything in between. Who could sleep with whom, why and how, varied widely with the social context. The bed witnessed many of these antics.

LIE BACK

The paintings on the walls of the chapel of the Egyptian vizier Mereruka's tomb, as recalled from chapter 1, show him holding his wife's hand as they approach a marital bed.[3] The consequence was no doubt sex, but the intent was conception. Sex was a deeply serious pastime for pharaohs and high officials in an era when sudden illness could take the ruler to eternity without warning. If he had no heirs, crisis could ensue. The court was a morass of plots and counterplots, of officials vying for favor, and all of the plotters had a large stake in events that occurred in the royal bed, where the pharaoh was tasked with breeding his successor. Duty followed him even when he was entwined with his naked wife. Egyptian tomb artists never hinted at sex except in the most formal manner, as befitting the dignity and high office of those buried in imposing sepulchers. We know of only one example of a hieroglyphic representation that depicts a couple having sex: it comes from a Middle Kingdom tomb at Beni Hasan, but has long been erased by visitors' curious touching. There are, however, many informal representations of sexual intercourse in graffiti as well as in a papyrus known as the "Turin Erotic Papyrus," which seems to depict a brothel containing various erotic props, including one in the form of a chariot.

Like every other preindustrial civilization (or at least all those whose written records have been deciphered), Egypt was organized around men. With possessions and land to pass on from father to son, the male line needed to be secure. The fact that women were having the children was an uncomfortable threat to the order of things. Women and their sexuality needed to be controlled. The wedding bed was an important means of control.

For the Sumerians of Mesopotamia marriage was a business transaction.[4] In their language the word for love meant "to mark off land." For a couple to be married, a contract was drawn up, families of the bride and bridegroom paying a dowry and bride price. Right after the wedding ceremony and marriage feast, the bride moved with her husband to her father-in-law's house. Sexual intercourse followed, with the expectation that the bride was a virgin and that she would become pregnant. If any of these stages were bypassed or not performed properly the marriage could be invalidated.

The Greeks and Romans formalized male and female roles in the marriage bed. Upper- and middle-class fathers, as heads of families, carefully arranged marriages for their daughters or used duly appointed guardians. Xenophon, in his *Economics*, has the witheringly pragmatic Ischomachus tell his fourteen-year-old bride, "We should have had no difficulty in finding someone else to share our beds" before concluding, "But I for myself and your parents for you considered who was the best partner of home and children that we could get. My choice fell on you, and your parents, it appears, chose me as the best they could find."[5]

Even a Roman girl's virginity was only one-third hers. The remaining two-thirds belonged to her parents, who passed her down to a future son-in-law with an appropriate dowry. A Roman wife's duties were onerous and began the moment she set foot in her husband's house. She was expected to be faithful and sexually virtuous, to conceive and bring up children, to take responsibility for the household, and to spin wool. A woman with a fecund marriage and a well-managed home was much honored. A *madrona* was a one-man wife, and her ultimate task was to have children, preferably boys, who would serve in the empire's military or civil administration and guarantee the survival of the family line. The first-century-BC poet Catullus wrote in a wedding poem that the wedding night should produce soldiers to man the frontiers. His more cynical contemporary Propertius bred children but flatly refused to let his sons become soldiers.

Women in Emperor Augustus's time had a legal status on a par with children and slaves. They were subordinate to their fathers, brothers, and husbands. Sex and procreation were wifely duties. How much they enjoyed these duties is a mystery, but often, especially for women who were weary of repeated pregnancies, it must have been a matter of lying on one's back and thinking of Rome. Sexuality was central to Roman religion and thus to the state. The lawyer and politician Cicero wrote of the reproductive instinct common to all living things, the union between husband and wife being "the foundation of civil government, the nursery, as it were, of the state."[6] Though daughters and sons were both subject to *patria potestas*, the power wielded by their father as head of the household, early imperial Rome did include some educated, "emancipated" women who, though unable to vote or hold political office (aside from the priestly office of the Vestal Virgins), could and did exert influence. Fresh from his divorce from his activist wife Terentia, Cicero was asked whether he would marry again. He replied that he couldn't cope with philosophy and a wife at the same time. He soon recanted because he had to repay Terentia's dowry, and the only way he could afford it was by marrying another woman.

Cicero and his wife, like all married couples in mostly affluent households, probably shared a bedroom. These were usually square, located on either the first or second floor, and looking out on an open courtyard. The windows were small, not necessarily for privacy but because Roman structural technology was generally simple, with stone lintels or modest brick arches. The main furniture was the bed, the only relatively secluded place in the house and used for sleeping and marital sex. Most good-quality beds were made of wood, the more expensive ones adorned with ornamental metalwork. They were generally of light construction, which means few have survived, and they are known to us mainly from friezes at Herculaneum and Pompeii and paintings or reliefs elsewhere. Roman beds were usually three-sided, open rectangular boxes on legs, the fourth (long) side being open for easy access. Some had slanted structures at the ends to support pillows. The *lectum* could be a humble piece of furniture, but it received considerable elaboration in wealthy households. Its ancestry lay in classical Greek beds and couches, which were of much the same design.

The status of medieval women in Europe varied considerably. Some, like Eleanor of Aquitaine (1122–1204), were wealthy and powerful, and others became powerful abbesses and administrators of religious communities. But husbands effectively held the power and control in marriage, despite many nuances, especially in affluent relationships. In Tudor England girls remained their father's property until they were their husband's property. When Sir William Roper called on the statesman Sir Thomas More early one morning to choose one of his daughters as his wife, More took him into his bedchamber, where his two girls were sleeping on a truckle bed. He threw off the sheet. The girls lay with their smocks up to their armpits. As they turned modestly onto their fronts, Sir William remarked, "I have seen both sides," patted one on the buttocks, and proclaimed that she was his. What the girls thought of this remains undocumented.[7]

In More's time the ceremonial bedding of elite newlyweds was a public spectacle for the court. In an era of arranged marriages that often had significant diplomatic consequences, consummation symbolized an unbreakable alliance. After the wedding feast, the bride would be undressed by her ladies and put to bed. Then the groom would arrive in his nightshirt, accompanied by his attendants and sometimes musicians and a priest to bless the union. The bed curtains were then drawn. Sometimes the witnesses would not leave until they saw the couple's naked legs touching. Often the onlookers would linger even longer, waiting to hear suggestive noises. Next morning, the stained bed linen might be displayed as proof of consummation.

Brides were expected to be virgins, but not all were. The methods used to produce convincing bleeding included the surreptitious wiping of a scrap of blood-soaked sponge around the vagina. More recently, nineteenth-century prostitutes in Europe and the United States, who could command more money by claiming to be (STD-free) virgins, were known to use fragments of broken glass or even bloodsucking leeches to stain the bedsheets.

According to conventional wisdom, the best-matched partners tended to be roughly similar in age, status, and wealth. Second marriages, however, sometimes involved partners of very different ages. After the fifty-two-year-old King Louis XII of France married Mary, the eighteen-year-old sister of England's Henry VIII, in 1514, he died in three months, apparently worn out by his efforts in bed. It is likely that few royal couples were so ardent, given that dynastic continuity was a far more important consideration than sexual attraction or romantic love. Nobility and royalty planned early: Prince Arthur of England (b. 1486) was two when he was betrothed to Katherine of Aragon, then three years old. In seventeenth-century England the word *bed* was so intimately bound with the idea of marriage that it formed part of its legal definition. *Bed* also served as shorthand to describe the state of the marriage. If a partner committed adultery, he or she was said to have defiled the other's bed, and the offended partner could "kick them out of bed."

∎

Traditional Chinese marriages were usually formally arranged, almost like real estate transactions. Intermediaries arranged the financial and social details, and the groom would visit the bride's parents only after the negotiations were over. After the visit the bride returned home with him. The wedding dinner was held the same day, after which the couple consummated the marriage in the "mysterious room," the bridal chamber. The bride was again expected to be a virgin, and proof in the form of a bloodied sheet was demanded the next morning. Many grooms presented their new wives with illustrated manuals that showed different positions for coitus. Once married, many women rarely saw their men except at mealtimes and in bed.[8]

In wealthy households bed curtains appear to have had important significance to wives, symbolizing their lifelong bond to their husbands. The wealthy invested in expensive silk bed hangings embroidered with motifs of celestial beings. These curtains created a chamber within the room, keeping out insects and cold as well as providing a degree of privacy in a large room where several people slept. A third-century-BC text, *The Admonitions of the Instructress to the Court Ladies*, depicts a canopy bed that is a platform on four legs with uprights supporting light fabric.

Chinese courtiers, like pharaonic officials, managed the emperor's sex life on a strict calendar. It was routine for the palace concubines to compete intensely for the emperor's favor, their access to him controlled by regiments of eunuchs. Once the emperor selected his concubines for the night, they were carried naked into the imperial chamber wrapped in a golden cloth and deposited at the foot of his bed. Each concubine would crawl under the bedclothes at the foot and make her way gently upward until she was level with the royal countenance. Emperors were said to be sex machines: apparently they often had sex with as many as nine women in one night, bringing each to orgasm after careful foreplay but never ejaculating themselves, which required great self-control. How much of this was fantasy remains unclear, and whatever the concubines' true physical feelings, they knew their role was to entertain and claim rapturous enjoyment. Bedding so many "orgasmic" women was ideal for the emperor's well-being: it was believed that vaginal secretions strengthened male essence (yang).

In addition to pleasuring concubines, the emperor, when there was a full moon, was expected to spend the night alone with the empress. Even then the court astrologer and royal physician would tell him the hour at which he should ejaculate to produce a male child. This formalized sex occurred on an impressive scale. The Yellow Emperor of China, the mythical founder of Chinese civilization, was said to have gained immortality by having sex with a thousand nubile virgins. Another emperor, Sui Yang To (AD 581–618), maintained three thousand palace maidens, sometimes used for sex, as well as over seventy concubines. He is said to have preferred his concubines or maidens to be teenage virgins. He did not take them to bed but had them placed in a wheeled chair that held their legs and arms apart. A mechanized cushion moved the girl into the right position "to gain the royal favor." The male obsession with inexperienced yet fertile young virgins appears again and again in patriarchal societies, understandable when we remember that men wanted to assure their progeny. Yet a virgin does not necessarily equate to much fun in bed if we are to assume that practice makes perfect.

∎

Victorian Britain, superficially the epitome of respectability and straightlaced behavior, was riddled with centuries of preconceived ideas and taboos. Sex was a forbidden subject, something engaged in purely to produce children and strictly in the privacy of one's bedchamber. Women were expected to be chaste, the ultimate Christian model being to replicate the Virgin mother. To be discovered to have fornicated for pleasure was a major stain on one's reputation. The penalties for transgressing boundaries were harsh and public, and the disgrace of "bastard" remained very real. Puritan teachings resonated through British and much of European society.

Masturbation, once a subject of comedic delight in Attic Greece, was now a forbidden practice, the prohibition enforced by ruthless devices like the penis ring, whose spikes would awaken the sleeper before his dreams developed. Under Henry VIII, anal sex, whether homosexual or heterosexual, was classified as "[being] against the Will of man and God" and carried the death sentence. By Victorian times male homosexuality was considered a disease, while female homosexuality wasn't even a possibility. Sexual education was unknown. The fictional Mrs. Grundy of Victorian times reinforced conventional attitudes to the bedroom as a place for procreation with as little pleasure as possible.[9]

Yet despite the patriarchal setup found within large-scale civilizations there were other cultures in which women were on top—or certainly equal to men—when it came to bedding down. As part of his trailblazing anthropological research a century ago Bronislaw Malinowski studied the Trobriand Islanders' sexual life. A matrilineal society, like the Hopi and Iroquois in the United States, the

Trobriand Islanders kept children and wealth in the mother's family.[10] Women were encouraged to be assertive and dominant in pursuing or refusing a lover. There was no formal marriage ceremony; instead the young couple slept in a bed together. If they wished to marry, the girl accepted a gift—yams were favored—from her lover. The girl's parents then accepted the marriage. Divorce was easy and a mutual decision. If the man wanted to get back with the woman, he wooed her with more yams and gift giving, but the decision to let him back into her bed was hers. Babies were believed to be the result of magic, specifically an ancestral spirit entering the woman's body. After the child was born it was the mother's brother who presented a harvest of yams to his sister, so the child would be fed with food from its own matrilineage. From the age of seven or eight boys and girls engaged in sex play as a way of learning about life with same-age friends. Actual sex began about four or five years later. Most villages had a special hut called a *bukumatula* that contained beds (not specifically described) for extramarital encounters. It wasn't all free-love anarchy, however. Malinowski was careful to describe the rules of such encounters, including that it was considered bad manners to watch another couple making love.

THE SACRED AND THE PROFANE

The Epic of Gilgamesh, the classic early Mesopotamian literary work, describes sex as one of the great pleasures of people living on earth. When Enlil, the god of fertility and wisdom, married the goddess Ninlil, their first night together was rapturous: "In the bed chamber, on the flowered bed [whose fragrance is] pleasant as the cedar forest, Enlil, the god of fertility and wisdom, copulated with his wife, feeling great pleasure."[11] Though marriage was arranged by the family, the Mesopotamians appreciated romantic love and left many songs about people falling deeply in love. "Sleep begone! I want to hold my darling in my arms," is the title of one love poem.

Mesopotamians clearly enjoyed sex but not always in bed. Mass-produced Sumerian terracotta plaques from the early second millennium BC are highly explicit. One depicts a woman drinking with a straw from a beer jug while a man penetrates her from behind and quaffs from a wine cup. This symbolized their performing oral sex on each other. *Coitus a tergo*, from behind, was popular, perhaps because anal sex was a common way of avoiding pregnancy. Plaques also show the partners standing and in the missionary position. According to one expert, these plaques were part of popular culture, accessible to men, women, and children.

Despite the rectitude of the Egyptian court, ordinary Egyptians had many phrases and words for sex, including the euphemistic "to sleep with," the enthusiastic "to enjoy oneself with," and the curse "may a donkey violate him!" They had none of our modern prudishness over showing the erect penis, a symbol of fertility. When nineteenth-century archaeologists excavated the Nile Delta port of Naukratis, they were horrified to discover hundreds of erotic figurines, many with enormous phalli. These were deemed unfit for display and hidden away in museum storerooms. Finds include a limestone statuette of Horus the child, his penis so vast that it overshadows his head like a giant banana parasol. Similar "Naukratic figures," as the excavators euphemistically called them, have since been unearthed from many other Egyptian towns of the Late Period (664–332 BC), particularly in the Nile Delta. They were almost certainly used in fertility rituals like the "festival of drunkenness," which celebrated the inundation of the Nile.

Roman writings also abounded with references to fun in bed. A celebrated Roman myth of Cupid, the god of love, and Psyche, the goddess of soul, tells of Psyche's love of her bed and of night and her dread of the day. She is betrothed to Cupid but is forbidden ever to see him. Carefully cosseted and prepared for her wedding night, she awaits her new husband in a bed swathed with fine fabric.

Every night thereafter she receives her husband in orgies of connubial bliss. She has sworn never to behold her lover in daylight. One morning, however, she succumbs to temptation, and Cupid flees, never to return. Even in arranged marriages you sometimes learn of great devotion from funerary inscriptions. The butcher Lucius Aurelius Hermia and his wife, Aurelia Philematium, both freed slaves of Greek origin who lived in Rome during the first century BC, met when she was seven, and they were together for thirty-three years. By chance, their mortuary relief survives, now in the British Museum. He wrote, "My partner who departed this life before me was pure of body and loving of spirit. She was the only one for me." She said of him, "He whom I lost, alas, was really and truthfully much more than a father to me."[12]

The Chinese were refreshingly explicit, almost dogmatic, about sex in the bedroom. Their sex manuals are catalogues of specific expectations and instructions. "The more women with whom a man has intercourse, the greater will be the benefit he derives from the act," wrote the Taoist philosopher Ko Hung in the fourth century AD.[13] The Tao doctrine "the Supreme Path of Nature" dominated Chinese thought and society for more than two thousand years. The fundamental philosophy behind Taoism was that long life and happiness resulted from people learning how to live in perfect harmony with nature. Everyone had to aim for a harmonious interaction of yin, a passive force, and yang, the active force. When linked closely, they propelled one's breath of life toward the Way, Tao. When people strayed from the Natural Path, they could be led back to it by disciplines of the body. One of the most important was sexual intercourse, which, as we've seen in the case of the emperors, produced the necessary interaction between yin and yang. Yin essence was the moisture that lubricated a woman's sexual organs, yang the semen produced by a man. Sexual intercourse was thus one of the ways to heaven. A flood of explicit sex manuals educated readers on how to achieve the ideal balance of yin and yang, which depended as much on women's enjoyment as men's.

Chinese sex handbooks were usually divided into six sections. After an introductory essay on cosmic issues and the significance of sex, the book moved on to foreplay, then to the positions and techniques of intercourse. Taoist teaching proclaimed that "man is born to lie facing downwards and woman on her back," but the manuals offered other alternatives. Subsequent chapters discussed the therapeutic value of sex, choosing the right women, and how a woman should behave during pregnancy. Everything revolved around yin–yang harmony. Women's yin essence was inexhaustible, whereas men had limited quantities of yang essence. Ideally, then, again like the emperors, they had to prolong intercourse for as long as possible. A work entitled *Secret Instructions of the Jade Chamber* proclaimed that a strongly built fifteen-year-old male could emit semen twice a day. A strongly built seventy-year-old could do so once a month.

As far as the act was concerned, wherever there were flat surfaces there was sex. Chinese beds were originally mats on which people sat and slept. Sleeping platforms became popular with the arrival of Buddhism, around AD 200, which brought with it the belief that the Buddha sat on a raised dais. The platform soon gained prestige as a seat for honored guests and high officials, and beds too became more elaborate. Well-stuffed cushions added comfort—and allowed inventive sexual positions. Given China's cold winters, sleepers also valued a warm bed. During prehistoric times people often lit a fire on a clay floor, then swept away the embers before laying out sleeping mats on the warm surface. By 100 BC many houses had a raised platform known as a *kang*, with a stove built underneath it. Womenfolk spent a great deal of time atop the kang during the day, and they were used for all sorts of activities, including sex.

∎

Hindu Indians also considered sex a religious duty, a pleasurable way of improving one's karma and gaining the hope of reincarnation of one's soul at a higher level. The *Karmasutra* appeared about 600 BC, when the merchant class were growing in importance, wealth, and awareness of their social status, leading them to seek correct behavior in both religious and social circles. Karma was an individual quest, something self-centered and often a matter of harsh realism. At the same time, this most famous of sex manuals appeared when Hindus realized there was far more to sex than merely flirtation and the mechanics of sexual intercourse.[14]

The anonymous writer of the *Karmasutra* was concerned as much with the tangled emotions of people in love as he was with mechanics. Unlike the clinical Chinese sex manuals, he identified four categories of love: a simple love of sex; addictions to different forms of sex, such as kissing or oral acts; love that involved strong, spontaneous mutual attraction between a couple; and one-sided love, in which one admires the beauty of the other. Love was on a different plane from sex. The Chinese manuals were concerned with what happened in bed, not with how to get there or with ways to please one's husband in asexual ways, a fundamental aspect of female behavior in the *Karmasutra*. The book identifies seven types of congress, ranging from sex between people in love to a nobleman's seduction of a servant. There are classifications of penis size and, most famously, a catalogue of positions. Today, you can even download an app for your phone that lays them out like a workbook. But the book itself placed considerable emphasis on pleasure and careful preparation. "In the pleasure room decorated with flowers and fragrant with perfumes, attended by his friends and servants," the man would receive the woman, then engage her in pleasant conversation before everyone left and they moved on to the main event.

The *Karmasutra* is an athletic manual for lovers. Many of its positions defy all but the most youthful and nimble partners, but most of them require a comfortable platform and the strategic use of cushions and pillows to set the woman's body at the best angle for penetration and satisfaction. One could argue, probably wrongly, that the *Karmasutra* is what brought soft pillows into the sexual equation. Its teachings, along with those of other manuals, circulated widely. Sheikh Nefzawi, the author of the sixteenth-century Arabic work *The Perfumed Garden for the Soul's Recreation*, solemnly worked his way through all the standard sex positions and ended up with just eleven. He remarked, apparently with good reason, that Indians had "advanced further than we in the knowledge and investigation of coitus."

The Greeks are remembered for their homosexual encounters. In most vase paintings the couple is shown not on a bed per se but standing, with one partner's penis between the other's thighs. There are also a few examples of anal intercourse. In most cases the sex takes place between an older man, who tends to make the advance and stands with a bowed head and shoulders, as if both cringing and begging. The younger partner is usually upright and is sometimes repelling the older man.

Pederasty was the love of a man for a boy who had passed the age of puberty but was not yet an adult. Few men in classical Greece had sex with other mature men, on beds or otherwise. Boys were preferred, though sex with a prepubescent was illegal. "The bloom of a twelve-year-old boy is desirable," wrote Straton, "but at thirteen he is much more delightful. Sweeter still is the flower of love that blossoms at fourteen, and its charm increases at fifteen. Sixteen is the divine age."[15] This echoed the classical view that pederasty was a branch of higher education. Socrates said it allowed the cultivation of moral perfection. Part of the love classical Greek men felt for other men may have lain in their low opinion of women. "Women are by no means inferior to men" a generous Socrates is reported to have said. "All they need is a little more physical strength and energy of mind."[16] Female homosexuality was likewise acknowledged among the Greeks, the island of Lesbos being the heartland. Such was the esteem in which homosexuality was held that Plutarch noted that in "Sparta love was held in such high honour that even the most respectable women became infatuated with girls."[17] Beds were part of the backdrop of Greek sexuality, but by no means the inevitable stage for it.

In Roman times it was not just men who went off with other men or, indeed, courtesans. Married women snuck off to bed with men too. In early imperial times Augustus brought adultery into the public domain by introducing penalties, including exile for both men and women, for an offense that previously had been a family matter. There was a loophole: visiting prostitutes was not a crime. The Senate was surprised to witness a sudden increase in applications to be put on the register of prostitutes, many from respectable women. How much sex people had is anyone's guess, but Rabbi Eleizer, residing in Palestine in AD 80, wrote a commentary on the Torah in which he prescribed the amount of sexual activity that was appropriate for different categories of men. Students and the unemployed could have sex every day; people who worked, twice a week; donkey drivers, once a week; camel drivers, once a month; and sailors, once every six months.

In medieval Europe common people slept in common spaces, usually on the floor or the ground. This did not necessarily affect the enjoyment or frequency of sex. The records of church courts open a window into the fascinating world of medieval sex, the church being responsible for laws regulating personal morality. Many cases involved people having sex in stables. This was, after all, where male servants often slept. A great deal of sexual activity took place in the open air, perhaps on long grass or in places where some comfort was possible. Only the privileged shared a raised bed. When the mythic eighth-century hero Beowulf visited the "great mead-hall" of the Danish king Hrothgar, he doffed his helmet and weapons and climbed onto the great bed. "The pillow received the countenance of the lord" as he slept surrounded by his warriors. Almost invariably medieval artists drew the sleeper half-sitting with his or her face and sometimes upper body exposed. This enabled them to show the subject's countenance as well as reflecting the sleeping habits of the day.

In Europe, where the church was a powerful force, medieval literature abounds with accounts of lusty priests who seduced women in the confessional, monks and nuns who met in secret liaisons on the hard beds in their cells and in other locales, and nobles who kept mistresses and seduced serving wenches. A study based on ecclesiastical records in eastern England, deliciously entitled "Naughty Nuns and Promiscuous Monks," concludes that much of this activity involved outsiders and that the ebb and flow of sexual misconduct was typical of human nature rather than anything unusual.[18]

Tudor England took a contradictory view of sex, stressing that female enjoyment was necessary for conception to take place, yet advocating that a woman should not show enjoyment. The only permissible position for a woman was on her back, with any other believed to carry the risk of conceiving a deformed child. In civilized society good sex often had to be bought or perhaps enjoyed outside one's marriage.

SEX SELLS

Roman men fornicated not only with their wives but also, once given their wives' tacit acquiescence, with mistresses and boys. But a wife caught in adultery joined the ranks of the fallen and stigmatized, which included actresses, dancing girls, prostitutes, and those forbidden to marry free citizens of Rome. Adulterous men received no punishment whatsoever, but a husband could kill a guilty wife with impunity. The view that a man but not a woman may commit adultery persisted down the centuries. English women did not win the right to divorce their husbands for adultery until 1923.

Buying sex was a long-established business in Greece and Rome. Visit Pompeii's notorious brothels, and you soon understand that here, as in brothels throughout the Roman Empire, sex was a production line.[19] The graffiti on their walls has generated a large (and mostly very dull) academic literature. "I screwed a lot of girls here"; "Sollemnes, you screw well": so read the brags of long-dead men, etched for eternity onto the walls of Pompeii's famous Lupanare, "the wolf's den." Its bawdy wall paintings depict women astride men, on all fours, and in groups, their clients fully entertained. Hedonistic fantasy sells, but the action took place in a strictly utilitarian setting designed to keep men from lingering. The Lupanare was a dismal factory for clients' sexual gratification. The prostitutes plied their trade in ten windowless, cramped, squalid rooms on the second floor, each separated from the antechamber by a curtain. A thin mattress filled with hay or straw covered a rough stone bed built against the wall. Most of the women who worked there are thought to have been slaves of Asian or Greek origin, people whose services could be had for cash, two loaves of bread, or half a liter of wine—paid, of course, to the owner. For the middle- and working-class Pompeians who comprised its customer base, a visit to the Lupanare must have held all the erotic pleasure of a modern trip to a fast-food restaurant. It satisfied a need with depressing efficiency.

Male and female prostitution being lawful, most Roman brothels were open seven days a week, twenty-four hours a day. Rome at one point had at least forty-five of them. Cicero remarked that men buying sex was good for the nation. Prices were kept low, so the

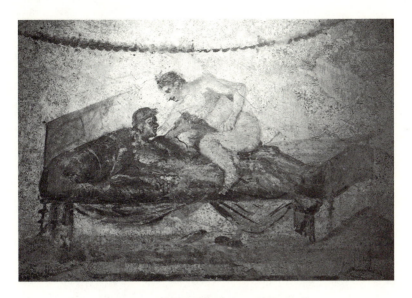

An erotic mural from the Lupanare, Pompeii.

ability to afford a whore was within the reach of every Roman. Paying for sex was as much part of a commoner's life as gladiator shows, games, and public baths. The beds were nothing more than stone shelves, but what did that matter when the act was over in moments? Some low-rent hotels, bars, and inns, called *noctilucae*, or "night lights," had tiny cubicles at the back with the necessary stone bed and straw mattress.

Chinese men were polygamous, and concubines were part of every affluent home. A wealthy man with multiple partners was well advised to behave rationally, to avoid causing trouble in the women's quarters. An anonymous fifteenth-century man told his son to concentrate his attention on the women already in the household rather than on the newcomer. The new girl, he said, should stand attentively by the ivory couch while he enjoyed the other women. After four or five nights, he might have intercourse with the newcomer, but the other women, including his concubines, had to be present.

In medieval Europe adultery was also part of polite society, provided one obeyed the unspoken rules. Apparently the ladies were as aggressive as the gallant knights, if not more so, though we get this from the admonishing remembrances of men, insisting that the women were oversexed and in need of control. As one disapproving nineteenth-century historian wrote of Sir Launcelot du Lac and Queen Guinevere, their behavior was "loose beyond anything that those who have not read these interesting records of medieval life can easily conceive."[20]

Male and female brothels flourished under Victorian Britain's respectable veneer. White slavers trafficked in both women and children. Some Victorian men patronized high-class flagellation establishments that indulged sadomasochistic fantasies, activities named after the Marquis de Sade and Leopold von Sacher-Masoch. These were powerful, concealed pleasures, accessible to Victorians with money and the right connections. Occasionally the providers became notorious.

Where there are large imbalances of power there is violence. Children during the Marquis de Sade's time were often treated harshly: "Do not spare the rod" was a typical Puritan sentiment. The childhood nanny would wield a whip, as did the schoolmaster. Many of the upper-class Victorian boys who came out of Eton, Westminster, Rugby, or any of England's best all-boy boarding schools had experienced sexually motivated violence.[21] No doubt aware of these masochistic patterns, Madame Theresa Berkely ran a well-equipped pleasure house in London's respectable Hallam Street in the 1820s and early 1830s. She was a dominatrix, a master of the art of inflicting pain and an expert in chastisement, flagellation, and whipping. Her Berkely Horse, a sloping board used for flogging, made her a fortune. Her talents were such that both aristocratic men and women sought her out, knowing she would inflict pain yet maintain their privacy. She also employed women who could be flogged by her clients. Berkely's toolkit included birches kept in water, which made them pliant, and even green nettles, which were said to restore "the dead to life." A slightly later brothel owner, May Frances Jeffries, ran several high-class brothels as well as a "flagellation house" in the respectable London suburb of Hampstead. Her customers were said to include the highest nobility.

While the sex props are endless in their ingenuity, the humble bed usually serves as the stage, as it has for sexual activities and fantasies since long before beds were elevated on legs. Despite its role, however, in the often-lively process of conceiving children the bed did not become the place where they are usually born until very recently.

FOUR

Call the Midwife

Nine months after the big bang of chapter 3 some women find themselves confronted with an even bigger bang: childbirth. In the modern West most give birth on their backs on a plastic and metal-framed hospital bed with a polyurethane foam mattress, sometimes rigged to monitors and pumped full of pain-relieving drugs. Although the technology is obviously very modern, the role of the bed is surprisingly new as well.

BIRTH BC

The group of hunter-gatherers who lived near Ostuni, Italy, around twenty-thousand years ago behaved unlike almost any other hunter-gatherers: they buried their dead in a cemetery. Among the interred was a woman in her late teens or perhaps a little older. Her wrists had been loaded with bracelets, of which only the hundreds of perforated shells remain, while more beads decorated her head. She lay on her left side with her right arm placed over her stomach. When archaeologists removed the earth around her pelvic region they found the whisper-thin bones of an almost complete fetus trapped between her legs. There is no doubt that the people who buried this woman tried to help her in what must have been a labor from hell. Unable to save her, they placed her in the ground, as if at rest, and covered her with rich ornamentation.[1]

Roughly twenty thousand years later some of us were told that such trauma was a result of Eve's fruit-based disobedience. "I will greatly multiply your pain in childbirth. In pain you will bring forth children," said the God of the Abrahamic religions.[2] In reality, it seems that evolution traded female pain and a few stuck babies for the greater good of all. Once our ancestors got up onto two legs, roughly six million years ago, the birth canal narrowed. Alongside this our brain / skull size gradually increased, so that among modern humans one in every thousand babies has a head too big to pass through the birth canal. Yet we've used these troublesome aspects—our big heads and our dexterous hands, freed up thanks to bipedalism—to support childbirth. Unlike most other animals, almost every human woman in labor has help. Sometimes this assistance can turn into a huge production.

For most of human history the bed was not the place for labor itself but a platform for recovering afterward. One of the very earliest representations of childbirth is a baked-clay statuette of an obese woman, probably some sort of fertility charm, that dates to roughly 5800 BC and was found buried in a grain bin in the early agricultural town of Çatalhöyük in modern-day Turkey. Measuring 16.5 cm (without her head, which was missing), the so-called Seated Woman of Çatalhöyük sits on a throne with feline-headed armrests and appears to be giving birth. No bed here, just a chair.[3] Birthing chairs, specifically, low stools, turn up in second-millennium-BC Mesopotamia too. Written records tell us that only after labor would a woman retreat to her bed, for thirty days of rest and isolation. For the rich this meant wood-framed beds raised off the ground, with woven mattresses and perhaps linen sheets, wool blankets, and plump cushions. Middling types might lie on bundles of reeds across a mud-brick platform topped with a woven reed mat, while the poor retreated to their reed mats.

This secluded bed-bound period was an excellent idea since it helped reduce postpartum contamination by others. According to the World Health Organization, 41 percent of all modern deaths among children under five happen in the first twenty-eight days of life, and 75 percent of those deaths occur in the first week.[4] But the Mesopotamians, not yet aware of germ theory, gave the reason for the mother's isolation as female uncleanliness. It was the women, not her visitors, who was said to be in an impure state, tainted by childbirth and blood. Only through exclusion and ritual could she be made clean again.

Beds played a similar role in postbirth purification, rest, and recovery in ancient Egypt. Only one text, a seventh-century-BC document known as Papyrus Brooklyn (47.218.2), describes a laboring woman lying down—perhaps (the text is unclear) on a bed or a mat of reeds. In all other cases women would stand, kneel, crouch, and use "birth bricks" or a stool. Even the hieroglyphic symbol for childbirth is a kneeling woman with the child's head and arms emerging from her body. A rare text from the workers' village at Deir el-Medina, across the Nile from modern-day Luxor, backs up this idea. It tells how a laboring woman would kneel on the ground, one midwife holding her upraised arms while a second would receive or pull the baby from her womb. This is exactly what we see on a relief from the temple of Esna, in Upper Egypt: the naked queen Cleopatra VII (69–30 BC) kneels with her arms up as one midwife supports her from behind and a second kneels before her holding up the queen's honorably enormous, toddler-sized baby. This icon goes back at least as far as the time of the female king Hatshepsut (mid-fifteenth-century BC), whose mother, Queen Ahmes, wife of Thutmose I, is similarly depicted.

While a woman might not necessarily use her bed as a platform for labor, some probably retreated to their bedrooms to give birth: the aforementioned Papyrus Brooklyn contains two protective spells for the bedchamber. Other women may have gone up onto the roof or into some sort of temporary shelter behind the house—there are a few divine scenes of mothers in labor in vine-covered arbors. The main thing is that women probably wanted isolation, which may not have been easy in small, crowded urban dwellings.

As in the case of sex, sleeping, eating, and mummification, the Egyptians stubbornly failed to record details of birth. Perhaps it was not interesting enough, or maybe information on how to handle labor was passed on verbally by (illiterate, female) midwives. One of the few texts to describe labor is the Westcar Papyrus, found in "mysterious circumstances" by the British adventurer Henry Westcar in the 1820s. Drafted by an anonymous scribe sometime in the sixteenth to eighteenth centuries BC, it tells five stories, concluding with the labor of the mythical woman named Reddjedet.[5]

"Reddjedet felt the pangs, and her labor was difficult," it ominously begins. So her husband, high priest of the sun god Ra, prays for help from the deities Isis, Meskhenet, Hekhnet, Nephthys, and Khnum. The goddesses arrive disguised as dancing girls and shut themselves in the room with Reddjedet. The woman then delivers triplet boys, who slip into the arms of the midwife Isis. As the future kings of a new dynasty, her infants miraculously emerge with gold-covered limbs the color of gods' flesh and wearing lapis headdresses, the hew of gods' hair. After the birth the scribe tells us how the queen was put in isolation and helped by females, including her servant girl, who somehow ends up getting eaten by a crocodile. Though Reddjedet's birth story reveals useful nuggets about labor and postbirth rituals, no bed is explicitly mentioned as part of her labor. It was probably more usual and convenient to give birth on a mat on the ground.

Once labor began, midwives would chant prayers, burn resin, and offer beer. Alcohol provided crude pain relief while also bringing the mother closer to the protective goddess Hathor, the Lady of Drunkenness. Sometimes midwives seem to have used hippo tusk wands carved with protective symbols and often with worn edges that hint at long-forgotten rituals.[6] After the baby was born, the midwife cut the umbilical cord with a tough reed or a special, often fish-shaped obsidian knife. Since the placenta was thought to represent the person's life force, it was saved, dried, and often buried, sometimes in the doorway to the house, a ritual that was still being observed in parts of early twentieth-century Egypt.

Medicine and magic were always closely bound. In ancient gynecological texts advice on how to deal with a prolapsed uterus appears alongside spells to ward off miscarriage. Like the Mesopotamians, Egyptian women were confined after birth, though for a less generous two weeks. From 1800 BC we find bed headrests decorated with images of the childbirth protectors Aha / Bes and Ipy / Taweret, who presumably guarded the woman's body. From 1450 BC, roughly a century before Tutankhamun, we find clay and stone figurines that may depict confinement: naked women with ornate wigs and jewelry lying in bed, often flanked by a child. The Deir el-Medina texts also say that paternity leave existed, and that men bought special items to help their wives, including custom-made beds with legs the shape of the dwarf god Bes. But once the fortnight was up, the woman and child left their beds to be reintroduced back into society with a timely celebration.

MAGIC AND MEDICINE

With the passage of time medical knowledge increased. In the sixth century BC the Indian physician Sushruta left stunningly detailed scientific records of normal pregnancy and birth as well as pathological deliveries.[7] Some of his findings may have influenced the Greeks. Magic still played a role in Greek medicine, however, and even Hippocrates's original fifth-century-BC oath contains incantations. There was also much pragmatism. Greek and Roman medicine decreed that if the fetus was assumed to be dead or stuck, then it had to be evacuated to attempt to preserve the mother's life.

Horrifying collections of obstetric instruments have been found from sites such as Pompeii's House of the Surgeon. Hooked knives were used to dismember a stuck fetus. The physician Soranus of Ephesus, of the first or second century AD, recommended that, to avoid harming the mother, parts of the fetus be amputated only as they presented rather than internally. [8] Very large heads were split or crushed with a craniocast—a bowed forceps with teeth. This may not have been met with too much outrage. Soranus tells of how once the child had been delivered it should be given to the mother after the grandmother or a maternal aunt had warded off the evil eye with a finger dipped in saliva. The father would then be brought to the bedside to decide whether the child should live or die. As the Athenian comic poet Posidippus wrote in the third century BC: "Everyone, even a poor man, raises a son. Everyone, even a rich man, exposes a daughter."[9] Unwanted babies could be abandoned, for example, at the Temple of Pietas, while deformed "monsters" were drowned or suffocated. In his *Politics* Aristotle advocated a law criminalizing the rearing of deformed or disabled children. Monstrosity was often blamed on the pregnant woman, who was thought to have looked at the wrong thing. Women were advised to contemplate fine statuary to ensure well-proportioned babies, whereas eyeing a monkey, for instance, would result in hairy offspring with long arms.

Like all major civilizations before and since, Greek and Roman society traced descent through the men. But since the women reproduced, they had the ability to disrupt the male system. For the patriarchal arrangement to work, women needed to be kept in line. Effective ways to do this included the time-honored method of asserting that postpartum women were polluted and unclean and by claiming that children were actually the work of men. Both the Greeks and the Romans considered women simply empty vessels through which a man's children were born, with no real input from the woman—unless there was a problem, such as too much monkey gazing.

Although these were male-led systems, care was given to women's health. Among the twenty medical books written by Soranus of Ephesus is one on gynecology. The originals have all been lost, but they were widely quoted by later writers. He recommended clean hands for midwives and promoted his version of pregnancy aromatherapy, which included asking women to inhale the scent of an apple or a clod of earth (making one realize how our ideas about fragrance have changed in the modern era). He prescribed three weeks of bedrest after the birth. The urban woman would retreat to her bed, or *kliné*, as it was known to the Greeks, a rectangular bed supported on four legs, two of which could be longer to support an armrest or headboard. Numerous pictures of *klinai* on vases show fabric draped over the couch's woven platforms and cushions placed against the headrest. Rich women could enjoy layers of intricately woven fabrics and beds heaped with pillows. Some new mothers employed a wet nurse, though Tacitus praises German women for nursing their own, which suggests that this was seen as virtuous but was spurned by those who could afford to do so. During the bed-rest period children would be named—on the eighth day for girls and on the ninth for boys—after the critical period of neonatal danger had passed. The idea of *not* taking bed rest was unthinkable, though if we are to believe Strabo's *Geography*, when an Iberian woman gave birth her husband took to his bed and *she* looked after *him*.

TENTS AND "GROANING CHAIRS"

Imperial China developed an intricate tapestry of highly involved regulations surrounding birth.[10] The rules about the role of the bed were equally complex. The first requirement was that in her final month of pregnancy a woman should set up a tent or arrange a hut. This would be her special birth quarters and must not simply be screens around her regular bed. Huan Xuan, a warlord of the fourth century AD, recommended that his concubine use his wife's old tent, which suggests they were distinct pieces of kit—and that he was the last of the romantics.

The tent or hut would be erected outside the house or within a room inside it, much like the arbor of ancient Egypt. Setting up your tent was a dangerous business. One medical text warned that "whenever making a birth hut . . . it is forbidden to place it on fresh-cut wheat stalks or under tall trees, great misfortune!"[11] Birth charts dictated the direction the hut should face and where the placenta should be buried. After the tenth century AD placement issues became so complex that the birth chart was often hung inside the birthing room. Once labor began, the family had to "move away the beds and tables, spread grass in three or four places on the ground, hang down ropes and tie them to wood to make a horizontal bar . . . to allow her to lean against it like a crossbeam," explains an early medieval Chinese text.[12] Again, squatting on the ground seems to have been the norm throughout much of history. As the fifth-century-AD doctor Chen Yanzhi wrote, "In ancient times, women gave birth by getting on the ground and sitting on the straw just like awaiting death."[13] Presumably the straw was spread on the ground ahead of time.

Female midwives would hold the woman by the waist from behind, probably the most common position in China before the twentieth century. Only if the mother became exhausted would she lie on the ground or on a bed. One text advises that where there are any complications those attending the birth should first "make the mother lie down in her bed," which suggests that when all was fine, women didn't use them. This advice may partly be due to the height of some of the beds: after the third century AD elite beds were sometimes far off the ground. One mother in the Southern Dynasties was said to have thrown herself from her bed to the ground in an attempt to abort a fetus, implying that her bed must have been of some height. This penchant for high beds may be related to Buddhism, which reached China around AD 200. The imagery of the new beliefs presented the Buddha sitting on a raised platform instead of just a mat, which led to a fashion for platforms as honorific seats for special guests, dignitaries, or officials. These soon became longer versions for resting, which evolved into raised beds.

The Chinese regarded birth as women's business, attended by female midwives. But if the baby's father did everything correctly according to the rules, then her successful labor was thanks to him. To magically cause the placenta and fetus to emerge at once, the dutiful man would take his clothes and cover a well with them. To ensure a safe birth he could feed his wife his charred and ground fingernail clippings or a concoction of his roasted pubic hair mixed with cinnabar paste. These recipes sound bizarre to us, but following them was considered vitally important. The physician Chen Yanzhi, of the fifth century AD, said that childbirth was like awaiting death on the ground. As soon as it was over, relatives would bring pig liver to celebrate. Depending on the family's wealth, the mother might also be given mutton, elk, or deer. Medieval Chinese doctors referred to the time directly after birth as "three days of life and death" and recommended that women "stay in bed propped up high, on their backs with the knees up," for "observation." Her polluted condition meant she had to stay in her bedchamber, in confinement, for thirty days. There was also a taboo on sex for a hundred days, lest the woman catch the diseases of the

Five Taxations and the Seven Damages, such as vaginal discharge. The ancient texts do not explicitly blame women for problems in childbirth, but, again, they indicate that women were impure and had to take numerous measures to prevent breaking taboos or offending the spirits.[14]

Other birth-related taboos appear throughout Europe. In Tudor times an English woman, as her final month approached, would take to her bedchamber. For several weeks she would sprinkle her bedsheets with holy water, close the windows, plug any keyholes, and draw the curtains against daylight. It was thought that difficult births could be caused by lurking devils or ignored superstitions, such as looking at the moon. She might be given folkloric remedies, perhaps sprinkling her belly with powdered ants' eggs. In premodern times people often based medical treatments on similarity of appearance between malady and treatment, which is why the crinkly walnut was eaten to help the brain—which it does, but this is entirely coincidental.[15]

Once labor began, it was a women-only event—even the word *midwife* is Old English for "with woman." The man's role was to go "nidgeting," that is, to call the midwife and the woman's close female friends and relatives. These were her "God-sibs," or "gossips." Their aim was to keep the mother calm, perhaps by telling her what was going on in the world outside her bedchamber. They might also perform old rituals, such as taking off rings or unfastening belts—thought to mimic strangulation and therefore potentially harm the baby—or offer charms like cowrie shells, which look a bit like vulvas and so were thought to bring good luck to that region.

As labor progressed, a woman might rest on a small, portable, wood-framed pallet bed, which could be moved to wherever she was. Or she might squat on the midwife's birthing stool, known as a "groaning chair." After the Protestant Reformation rather more groaning went on, as pain relief was made illegal. One midwife was burned alive in 1591 for using opium to assist labors. Many of the old Catholic ways—the charms, the statuettes, the remedies, and the incantations—were also banned as superstitious. Yet after the Catholic Queen Mary came to the throne in 1559 many of the embargoed objects reemerged, suggesting that perhaps they never really went away.[16] But now most women, at least officially, had to rely on herbs, prayer, and their gossips.

Even though many mothers had special childbed linen, often family heirlooms given at marriage that were brought to the laboring mother, the blood-soaked act of birth itself usually took place on rags or old soft linen. The rich might retreat to the master bedroom; lesser folk would go to an area partitioned off for privacy, maybe near the central fire. After the event the midwife would clean the baby. A prince might be washed in wine, his skin rubbed with butter, and his navel dusted with a mix of powdered aloe and Arabian or Abyssinian frankincense.

In Tudor times the new mother, regardless of status, was known as a "green woman" and regarded as unclean, tainted by sex and delivery. During her confinement she was not allowed to look at the sky or the earth or even meet another's eyes, and sex was strictly forbidden. To reestablish her social and moral identity, after the month was up she would be "churched." For the ceremony she would be veiled and led from her bedchamber to the church porch, as though in marriage, to be given near-virginal (clean) status. If she was too unwell to go to the church, the priest might visit her at home.

Women knew well the dangers of childbirth. Pregnant women often had their portraits painted for posterity, just in case. In fifteenth-century Florence most women wrote their wills as soon as they knew they were pregnant. Even the richest queens were not immune but, in fact, more vulnerable than most. There could be up to seventy people in the royal bedchamber when a future monarch was born, which put them at increased risk of "childbed fever" (puerperal fever), a germ-borne disease usually spread by dirty hands or smocks. Two of Henry VIII's wives—Jane Seymour and Katherine Parr (giving birth in her second marriage)—died this way after an anxious court crammed into their bedrooms. It is hard to be sure of more general maternal death rates, but a sixteenth-century case study of the Aldgate area in London suggests a rate of 2.35 deaths per 100 pregnancies.[17] Given that women could have upward of seven children, this means that roughly 1 in every 7 mothers ultimately died in childbirth.

The numbers attending a birth could also get quite high in colonial America. A Puritan woman might have over ten people in her bedchamber, including her midwife, her mother-in-law, and a few neighbors. The master bedroom or perhaps the kitchen, depending on wealth and circumstances, would be the preferred places to give birth, quite likely on a bed of straw, which would then be burned after the birth. Around 1760, however, upper-class American women started to demand doctors at their births.

BIRTH ON THE BED
The switch to birthing on the bed can be traced back to sixteenth-century France and the emergence of modern obstetric surgery. An obstetrician now required the woman to lie back on a bed so that he could literally "stand before" her (from the Latin) to use his medical equipment. (We write "he" and "his" because all obstetricians were initially male barber-surgeons.)

Until the eighteenth century obstetricians' work was seen as indecent, and their social standing was on a par with carpenters and shoemakers. In entering a traditionally female domain these men found themselves in fierce competition with the female midwives. To gain leverage the obstetricians developed a new disease-oriented view of childbirth. Birth had always been seen as a dangerous event but never before as a disorder. Now, however, the new surgeons set out to convince women that pregnancy was an illness and that it required her to lie in bed, like an invalid. This made his implement-wielding presence not only appropriate but essential. The mother would passively lie back, and through his skills he would actively deliver her baby.

The new ideology took root quickly. In 1598 one of France's pioneering obstetricians, Jacques Guillemeau (1550–1613), wrote in his influential text *Childbirth, or The Happie Deliverie of Women* that reclining on a bed was the best position to make women comfortable and speed labor. In 1668 the obstetrician François Mauriceau, a surgeon under Louis XIV, published *The Diseases of Women with Child and in Child-Bed*. His book reflected the now-popular view of pregnancy as an illness needing to be cured by men, with the bed as the platform. "The Bed must be so made," Mauriceau wrote, "that the Woman being ready to be delivered, should lie on her Back upon it, her Head and Breast a little raised so that she be neither lying nor sitting; for in this manner she breathes best, and will have more strength to help her Pains than if she were otherwise, or sunk down in her Bed."[18]

The bed was established as the correct setting for labor. Yet something more bizarre may have been at play in getting pregnant women on their backs. Mauriceau's king, Louis XIV, apparently enjoyed watching women in labor. Frustrated with the way the traditional birthing stool obscured his view, he is said to have promoted the new reclining position. The true influence of Louis is unknown, but given the Sun King's almost godlike status the story is entirely possible. Whatever the case, by the end of the seventeenth century the bed was the usual place to give birth in France for all but rural peasant women.

Among the developments obstetricians promoted were the forceps, advanced by the Chamberlen family in the early seventeenth

A woman giving birth in the eighteenth century.

century. The Chamberlen forceps were designed with a cephalic curve to fit around the baby's head, though lacking the pelvic curve of modern forceps. Their workings remained a family secret until the 1690s, when Hugh Chamberlen revealed the truth. Yet as long as the forceps remained unknown, the skills of the Chamberlens, who carried out deliveries under a bedsheet or blanket, must have seemed almost magical. At first such implements were regarded with suspicion, and midwives fought back against overzealous forceps-wielding physicians. But midwives eventually began to look like something from a superstitious, bygone era. In 1899, when Joseph Bolivar DeLee opened the Chicago Lying-in Hospital, he argued that childbirth was a medical process that had no place for midwives. He also championed beds for births, with pain relief and forceps delivery.

SICK BIRTH BEDS

Despite DeLee's insistence on the superiority of the hospital bed, at first such beds were anything but happy. During the eighteenth century Paris's original lying-in hospital, the Hôtel-Dieu, had twelve hundred beds and a large maternity section. Yet demand out-stripped availability, and women were often forced to share beds, sometimes giving birth side by side. The hospital suffered frequent epidemics of childbed fever, with death rates between two and eight per hundred deliveries, or around ten times the rate outside hospital. Women would suddenly run a fever, have pain, swelling, and blood loss in their abdomens, and succumb within days. No one had any idea what caused puerperal sepsis, but some thought it was mothers' milk gone bad. The Hôtel Dieu perpetuated this hypothesis in 1746 after one of the first documented hospital epidemics of childbed fever. When staff dissected the dead women's bodies they saw what they believed to be "clotted milk" clinging to the intestines and elsewhere, but it wasn't milk, it was pus.

Other doctors had different ideas—though the fault always lay with the woman. Perhaps she had worn tight petticoats in early pregnancy or else her vaginal fluids had poisoned her. No one guessed it was the fault of the doctor, going from patient to patient and unwittingly carrying bacteria on his instruments or hands, until Ignaz Semmelweis mounted an impassioned and ultimately futile campaign to get doctors and medical students at the First Maternity Clinic of the General Hospital in Vienna to wash their hands before examining patients. Often doctors would go straight from an autopsy to the examining room. Semmelweis failed to convince his colleagues despite bringing about a massive reduction of the death rate in his clinic. The physician and poet Oliver Wendell Holmes led the American campaign to stop the spread of the disease by urging doctors to wash their hands before attending to bed-bound women, but he too faced strong resistance. Doctors are gentlemen, asserted Charles Meigs of the Jefferson Medical College in Philadelphia, and "a gentleman's hands are clean."[19]

The nineteenth-century British obsession with avoiding any hint of sexuality extended into obstetrics. When Queen Victoria was crowned in 1837 male doctors could be present at a birth, but they were not supposed to look at their patients, only touch them—sometimes blindly feeling around for the baby beneath many layers of bedsheets. Later, the most common position among Victorian women when attended by a male doctor was to lie on the left side with knees bent and drawn up to the abdomen, a contortion that prevented doctor and patient from seeing each other's faces. Among aristocratic families there was even a fashion for special portable beds just for giving birth. Delivering the baby on a separate bed from the marital one was felt to diminish the sexual connotations of birth.

Soon, however, the very nonsexual, sanitized hospital bed, with its metal frame and stiff sheets, beckoned for more and more women. Medicine was radically transforming. Among the breakthroughs was Joseph Lister's pioneering of antisepsis in the 1860s, which ensured sterile surgery and made reused, bloodstained bed linen a thing of the past. This came on the heels of James Simpson's use of chloroform in 1847, whose miraculous pain-numbing benefits he supposedly discovered after a night of self-experimentation. Chloroform was given to Queen Victoria for her eighth labor, in 1853; she described the drug as "delightful beyond measure." Its use for general anesthesia in obstetrics skyrocketed.

MODERN BED BIRTH

By the mid 1930s more births in the United States took place in a hospital than outside it. Minutes after the baby was born, it would be carried off to a large central newborn nursery and placed in a clean, metal-framed crib. The baby would then be brought to its mother in assembly-line fashion for feeding every three to four hours, a very doable proposition thanks to the development of purportedly superior infant formula.

Despite the scientific advances, until the end of the 1930s one pregnancy in two hundred still led to the death of the mother. It was only with the development of antibiotics in the 1940s that the death rate plummeted. *Homo sapiens'* big brains and dexterous hands had achieved the unthinkable: finally, humans had seemingly triumphed over nature. By the late twentieth century childbirth had moved almost entirely out of the home and onto the hospital bed. The change was profound: in 1900 about 5 percent of American women delivered in hospitals; in the 1920s this rate had reached roughly 65 percent in some large US cities, rising to 95 percent in 1955. It stood at almost 99 percent around 2020.

Pregnant "patients" now undergo batteries of tests, and around one-third of all new mothers in both the United States and the United Kingdom undergo major baby-extracting surgery in the form of the caesarean section. Pliny the Elder claimed that an ancestor of Julius Caesar was delivered in this way. In reality, the name probably comes from the Latin *caedere*, "to cut," or from the Roman law Lex Caesarea (imperial law) that stated a woman who died in late pregnancy should be delivered soon after her death, part of a cultural taboo against mothers being buried pregnant. Before the developments of asepsis and anaesthesia, a caesarean birth almost certainly spelled death for the mother. Now, however, the obstetrician's hospital bed is the first bed most of us encounter.

Around eighty thousand North American women deemed to have high-risk pregnancies are directed to stay in bed for weeks before they go into labor. Some suggest this is nothing more than a "bed rest hoax" and that extended rest does not alter the final outcome and may actually harm the woman's mental health.[20] As for laboring on our backs, a recent meta-analysis showed that when women adopt so-called alternative positions, such as crouching or standing, their hospital labors tend to be shorter, with fewer caesareans and epidurals. A 1961 survey revealed that only 18 percent of women in preindustrial societies lie flat to give birth; as we've seen, this probably reflects historical practice in the West as well. And the midwives are still fighting back: the Royal College of Midwives in the United Kingdom entitled its 2010 report "Get her off the bed."

When it comes to new life, the bed has gone from being a place for active recovery to a place for passive birth, a transition that coincided with the switch from exclusively female midwives to largely male obstetricians—today 85 percent are male. Like every patriarchal society before us, ours largely attributes successful births to men. Another change, however, is that the bed is no longer a zone of female pollution. Now that we have overcome many childbirth illnesses, few women take an "unclean" month off in bed. Instead, women are instructed to emulate media-created celebrities who jump around in their jeans just days after delivery. This may be no better for female mental health.

In the early 1970s feminists argued that birth-related care needed to be demystified and women's lives demedicalized. They argued that childbirth is not a disease and most deliveries do not require hospitalization, and they championed a revival of the lay midwife. Their advocacy of home births led to bitter conflict with the medical profession. Although no US state forbade delivering at home, doctors who participated in home births were threatened with loss of hospital privileges and even their medical licenses. Things have changed a little, and today midwives attend some 8.2 percent of births in the United States, compared with only 1.1 percent in 1980.

Yet it is clearly thanks to modern medicine that humans have never been so safe. This is why 99 percent of modern-day Western women go willingly to the hospital bed. In so doing almost all can avoid the fate of the decorated young girl at Ostuni, or Arjumand Banu the exalted Indian queen who died having her fourteenth child in 1631 and is commemorated by the Taj Mahal, or indeed Charlotte Brontë, who died of hyperemesis gravidarum (chronic vomiting, weight loss, and dehydration) resulting from her advanced pregnancy in 1855, among many others. The postpartum bed was a place where life could easily morph into death.

FIVE

Death and Beyond

Around AD 450 a black-haired Moche woman died in her mid- to late twenties. She was buried wrapped up in hundreds of yards of cotton cloth and covered with a woven cane mat, probably her bed in life. Her well-preserved, naturally desiccated body still has folds of loose skin around her belly, suggesting she had given birth at least once. The archaeologists who discovered her concluded that she probably died from the complications of childbirth.[1]

Her extremely rare untouched tomb was discovered in 2006 at the top of the otherwise heavily plundered mud-brick pyramid of Cao Viejo, part of the El Brujo pyramid complex on the northern coast of Peru. Nicknamed the Lady of Cao, she was buried with a curious mix of traditionally female and male grave goods, including gold jewelry, gold sewing needles, weaving tools, two ceremonial war clubs, and twenty-three spears. Was she a powerful female leader, or perhaps the wife of a ruler who had given her the military items? Lacking written records, we can't know. What is certain is that she was an important person. Alongside her massive bed-bundle lay a handful of other bodies, including that of a teenage girl between the ages of seventeen and nineteen, a rope still around her neck, possibly a sacrificial guide to the afterworld.

But why, given her elite status and her lavish death offerings, was the Lady of Cao buried wrapped in a simple cane bed? Perhaps her sleeping mat was simply a practical way of containing her enormous funeral bundle, but perhaps it was also meant to provide security for her final journey. A recent survey revealed that 70 percent of modern westerners would prefer to die in their own beds—a wish that goes unfulfilled for the 50 percent who expire on the same sort of sanitized hospital bed on which they were born. The desire to die in one's own bed reflects the enduring connection between sleep, death, and the imagined afterlife. As far back as c. 2200 BC, in one of the world's earliest literary compositions, Gilgamesh invokes this link between sleep and death, saying to his lifeless friend, "Now what is this sleep which has seized you? You have turned dark and do not hear me!"[2]

Whenever archaeologists find human burials, the bodies tend to be positioned as if in sleep: stretched out on their backs or sides or curled up in the fetal position. A jumbled or awkward position, showing that the body was dumped and allowed to lie as it fell, is reserved for enemies, miscreants, and the dehumanized, such as the fifty-four mostly decapitated Vikings hurled into a burial pit at Ridgeway Hill in Dorset, southern England. Upside down or seated burial is extremely rare, though it does occur, for instance, among the elite of the Sican culture of coastal Peru during the ninth to fourteenth centuries AD.

Most of us maintain this sleep–death–afterlife connection. "Rest in peace" or "Sleep tight," we say. In the Old Testament one of the words for bed is the same as the Phoenician and Ugaritic word for coffin (*mskb*), and the Welsh word *bedd* means both a bed and a grave. The traditional Nuer pastoralists of the Nile believe that during sleep the soul wanders among the ancestors and that death occurs if the body awakens before the soul returns. We cannot be sure they are wrong. This lack of knowing makes us surround death with more rituals than any other human event. In this drama the bed consistently takes center stage, even if it means dragging a dying monarch into his bed for a last, formal farewell.

RITUALS AND SPIRITS

For the Mesopotamians, who left us the oldest written accounts of funerary rituals, the deathbed was of profound importance. Once it was clear that a person was dying, she or he would be moved to a special funerary bed, around which family and friends would gather. An empty chair would then be placed to the left of the bedstead. This was where the soul would sit after death while the body was washed, anointed with oil or perfume, and its mouth tied shut. Incense would be burnt. The corpse would be laid out on the bed alongside grave goods, perhaps some favored possessions, gifts for the gods, food, drink, and sandals.

Sandals were essential for the soul's journey to the afterlife, although the superrich preferred going by cart, for the trip was arduous. First, the spirit had to cross the demon-infested steppe to the west. Then it would be ferried over the infernal river Khubur, where it would finally be welcomed by a god who would tick off its name against a master list of humans. Once ensconced in the netherworld, the soul led a rather dreary existence, punctuated only by the occasional food offering from a relative. The one exception was for stillborn babies, who were said to spend their eternities playing games and eating honey.

Friends and family back on earth would enter a period of mourning: letting even the poorest person die without support was a sign of the greatest disrespect. Appropriate mourning behavior included dressing in sackcloth, wailing loudly, and scratching one's body.

Professional mourners, often prostitutes, might be hired, and a drum would be loudly beaten. Funerals were expensive, and in payment burial officials expected to receive the funerary bed and chair plus the clothes in which the person had died as well as grain, bread, and beer. In the mid-third millennium BC Irikagina of Lagash in Sumeria put his foot down and limited the number of funerary goods. He reduced beer jars from 7 to 3 and bread loaves from 420 to 80 and allowed only one bed and one head-support per funeral, adding that the bed must be removed from the grave after burial.[3] Mesopotamian funerals, not unlike today's weddings, were clearly ripe for commercial exploitation, especially given the belief that if the body was not buried properly then the ghost could return to haunt the living. This was why Mesopotamian victors always buried their enemies, even in battle.

Irikagina's rule against leaving beds in tombs implies that this was something people used to do. Bed burials are well attested on the other side of the Red Sea. As early as 4000 BC people in Egypt and Nubia (modern Sudan) buried their dead on bedlike stretchers, or biers, made of woven wood as well as on household beds. When the American archaeologist George Reisner excavated at Kerma, the capital of the Nubian kingdom of Kush, in the early 1900s, he found numerous bed burials dating to around 1700 BC.[4] The most common deathbed was made of wood, sometimes with legs shaped like those of cows and often with a webbed mattress. At times the beds had signs of wear, suggesting they had been the person's bed in life. Although Reisner found more graves with beds than without, such burials were still probably possible only for the rich who could afford to lose their beds. In modern Sudanese funerals people still carry their dead to their graves on beds, but they usually take the beds back home after a period of ritual purification.

The deathbed was also integral to the ancient Egyptian funeral. When Tutankhamun died in the late fourteenth century BC his tomb remained unfinished, but the walls of his burial chamber were painted with scenes of his funeral procession.[5] Twelve mourners in white tunics pull a sledge carrying a wooden bed bearing his mummy. His bed is covered with a shrine decorated with "festoons of garlands," as his discoverer, Howard Carter, put it. Tutankhamun's burial party would have dragged the mummy from the king's mortuary chapel at the edge of the desert overlooking the Nile, where his body had probably been embalmed, to the tomb. Behind his bed a procession of servants carried all the other goods he would need in the afterlife, including the canopic chest containing his internal organs, clothing, food, jewelry, and furniture. Such processions would be accompanied by a crowd of mourning women, sometimes hired and suitably disheveled, with wild hair, bare breasts, and waving arms.

Once the group reached the tomb entrance the mummy would be subjected to the final funerary rituals, usually carried out by the eldest son. Since Tutankhamun died at the age of nineteen and had no living heirs, his successor Ay, possibly his grandfather and potentially a shady character, performed the most sacred of these rituals: the Opening of the Mouth. In this ceremony the mummy was magically brought back to life to receive food, drink, and light— food and light in the tomb being two key elements needed for the afterlife. Ay, wearing leopard-skin robes, would have recited spells while touching the mummy's eyes and mouth with special tools, including a fishtail-shaped knife of the type used to cut newborns' umbilical cords, so perhaps eliciting ideas of birth and rebirth at death. The ritual touching at these ceremonies seems to have been quite forceful, according to research on fifty-one mummies by the Swiss Mummy Project, which revealed fractures and chips on many of their front teeth.[6]

Tutankhamun was placed in nested coffins that were in turn laid upon a gilded bed, described on Carter's index card as a "heavy wooden bed-shaped bier" that was "of concave form to receive the convex bottom of the anthropoid outer coffin."[7] It was elegantly crafted with two lion heads at the top, tails at the bottom, and legs made to look like the lion's front and back feet. The base has imitation webbing to look like a tight mattress, all in gold, while its underside is varnished black. This was a bed fit for a king and god. Golden shrines were erected around it, the tomb was then filled with treasure, and the door was sealed.

King Tutankhamun, as a former god on earth, would have spent his afterlife alongside his fellow gods, though the anticipated details of which remain obscure. For "ordinary" Egyptians, death was conceived in terms of going to another country known as the Field of Iaru, a happy place where people would live forever in perfect health. The poor would simply be buried in the desert, perhaps with an amulet or two, while in some periods the rich might be interred with extensive offerings and furniture. Such was the case for Kha, the architect of the tombs of Kings Amenhotep II, Thutmose IV, and Amenhotep III (fifteenth–fourteenth centuries BC), whose previously untouched tomb was found over a century ago in the workmen's community at Deir el-Medina.

Kha was buried with his wife, Meryet, and in addition to copious jewelry, garments, furniture, food, and Kha's collection of sixty triangular male bikini briefs, each had a beautiful bed. His was made of wood, with legs suggesting those of a lion and a tightly woven mattress. It didn't quite fit into the tomb chamber, but rather than take it back home the people who brought him there left it in the antechamber passage just outside the door. It probably wasn't commissioned for the tomb, but it was Kha's bed in life. Meryet's bed was similar to Kha's but smaller and painted white. Hers was made up with sheets, fringed bedcovers, towels, and a wooden headrest encased in two layers of cloth.[8] These beds were clearly significant to their owners and were probably also the platforms used to carry their bodies to the tomb.

OPULENCE IN DEATH

A good deathbed was an excellent way of communicating ideas of one's status on earth and in heaven. Few cultures took this symbolism to such extremes as the classical Greeks. Given that reclining on a dining couch, or *kliné*, while eating was a highly refined activity in Greek society, it was only a matter of time before the elite were actually burying their dead on such beds. Though the funerary dining couch turns up in earlier cultures, including in a second-millennium-BC tomb from Jericho, by the fifth century BC, the kliné deathbed was the most common icon on Greek funerary vases.[9]

We have little archaeological evidence for *klinai* deathbeds. Perhaps this is because their wooden frames have long since perished, or conceivably such beds were not normally left in the tomb. A fifth-century inscription from the island of Keos in the Aegean Sea states that both the bed and its covers must be returned home after the funeral. Among the rare examples in which people disregarded this advice are several graves in Kerameikos cemetery in Athens, which contain apparent traces of luxury wooden klinai inlaid with Near Eastern–style ivory, amber, and bone decorations. To be buried on such a couch must certainly have helped to define one as entitled to an afterlife of endless feasting.

The classical Greek love of the kliné in death may therefore be linked with changes in their perceptions of the afterlife.[10] In Homer's *Odyssey*, from the late eighth century BC, the Greek view of the hereafter was like that of the Mesopotamians: the spirit lived a dull, unchanging life in Hades, a dark underground place encircled by water. Only those whose bodies had been buried could cross the water and enter Hades, and the many-headed dog-monster Cerberus ate any who attempted to leave. There was no reward or punishment for how you had behaved in life. By the Archaic era (eighth to sixth centuries BC), Hades had become pleasanter, but in the classical period (fifth to fourth centuries BC), the idea of Elysium, or Paradise, began to take off and, with it, the use of the kliné as deathbed.

Despite its pleasant nature, the dining deathbed still required serious rituals. First, a close female relative, aged sixty or more, was tasked with anointing, washing, and clothing the corpse. Then the body was placed on the kliné, its head on a pillow and its feet pointing toward the door. Vases show men approaching the kliné with their right hands raised, while women duly beat their heads and breasts. Sometimes female musicians are shown playing the harp, flute, or lyre, but by the classical era professional mourners were no longer encouraged. Yet the beds persisted.

There was a fashion among elite Etruscans to be buried in terracotta coffins modeled into dining couch scenes. The Sarcophagus of the Spouses, which dates to the late sixth century BC, is one of the great masterpieces of Etruscan art. It depicts a married couple banqueting together with jolly faces and long, braided hair, all divinely fashioned from clay. In the wife's left hand is a small, round object, perhaps a pomegranate, a symbol of immortality. Etruscan women seem to have enjoyed more liberty compared to some of their contemporaries, and here she is, relaxing comfortably at her husband's side. In the Greek world banquets were reserved for men. Later, the kliné deathbed appears wherever the Greeks and Romans went—though, as in the case of the Etruscans, usually with a local spin. Given that Alexander the Great journeyed all the way to the Indus River, in modern Pakistan, it is unsurprising to find images of a dead Buddha lying on a Hellenistic- or Roman-style couch, with lathe-turned legs, in the local Gandharan-style art.

In the West the funeral kliné largely went out of style with the fall of the Romans, although we do find some sixteenth-century tomb figures resting with one arm on a couch. Yet such furniture only reappeared commonly in Victorian times, when the British, riding on the waves of their own empire, brought everything classical back into fashion. Aspirational Victorians sometimes went in for post-mortem displays in the parlor, laying their dead relative on a classical-style kliné: the chaise longue, or "fainting couch." Though the banqueting element had gone and the Victorian couch was now more associated with women than with men, the notion of luxury at death remained.

SURROUNDING THE BED

In many cultures the deathbed itself was a thoroughly social place where friends, family, and others would gather, often in large numbers. An audience was particularly critical when a dying person, for instance, the head of a household, was due to transfer status. Chinese emperors liked to have very public deaths. They aimed to speak the names of their preferred successors just before they died, in an attempt—not always successful—to prevent quarrels over the succession. There were unexpected hazards, too. On his deathbed the Chinese emperor Wenxuan of northern China (AD 526–59) took an elixir said to promote long life. It killed him.[11] He was in good company: various elixirs had killed a long list of Chinese emperors and high officials, including the Jin emperor Aidi, who died in AD 365, at the age of twenty-five, after taking a potion that accidentally fulfilled its promise that the taker would never grow old. At least Wenxuan had the sense to try his brew when he was about to die anyway.

Indian maharajahs tended to choose and adopt their heirs while on their deathbeds, a sensible move in volatile states where an adoptive son, if selected earlier, might decide to accelerate his inheritance. The deathbed assumed great importance amid intense speculation about the possible successor.

When Queen Elizabeth I died in bed in 1603 at the age of sixty-nine, relatively few people were in attendance. According to her maid of honor, Elizabeth Southwell, the problems started after the dying queen asked for a "true looking glass."[12] Every state-controlled portrait of the Virgin Queen showed her as an immaculate beauty with a perfect complexion, despite her having suffered from a bout of skin-scarring smallpox and rotten teeth. She was so horrified by what she saw in the glass that she banished from her chamber all those who had flattered and misled her.

The diminished crowd of onlookers on the day of her death nonetheless included her ladies in waiting, her doctor, her chaplains, the archbishop of Canterbury, and members of her Privy Council. Prayers were uttered, and as she teetered on the cusp of death she was asked if she agreed to King James of Scotland as her successor. Unable to speak, she simply raised a hand in agreement. Such were the rumors surrounding the queen's virginity and whether or not she had borne children that she left strict instructions that her body should not be disemboweled or examined, as was customary. Instead, she was placed directly in her coffin, which was in turn laid on her bed, where it was guarded by her ladies-in-waiting. The bed itself was covered in black velvet and decorated with huge ostrich plumes. Following a medieval tradition, a lifelike wooden effigy of the queen was then placed on the coffin. The effigy was a stand-in until the next monarch took the throne, and it remained there until her burial.

Echoes of this royal death resounded throughout Europe. In 1715 Louis XIV died as he had lived: in public and in his state bed. So important was the king's bed to French courtly life that even when it was unoccupied people entering the bedchamber would genuflect toward it as if it were an altar. Two days before he died Louis XIV still conducted affairs from there, including securing his great-grandson as his heir. His close domestic staff stayed by his bedside while many passed through his bedchamber, including the doctors checking his gangrenous leg, his family, courtiers, and other onlookers.

After the king's death various rooms in the palace were draped in black, but, in a departure from tradition, Louis XIV did not have the usual funeral effigy. The custom in France had been to commission a wicker effigy of the king (the English used wood) upon which would be fixed a wax mask and wax hands molded from the dead king's body. This doppelgänger would then be dressed and seated upon the state bed to receive visits. It would partake in a meal, where it would be served as though it were the living king. Such effigies were displayed prominently in the funeral procession, and people would flock to see them, but Louis XIV's father, Louis XIII, ordered the practice ended in 1622, arguing it was far too pagan.

Gathering around the deathbed was important not only for royals. The deathbed was a social place where friends and family would gather to support the dying person—and one another. In Elizabethan England, after a death the corpse would usually be washed and shrouded and maybe, if money allowed, crudely embalmed. The body would be placed on a bier or open coffin, often upon the person's bed. A watching period then began, as friends and family ensured that the body was never alone until its burial. This tradition was quite common until the middle of the twentieth century.

Catholics considered it important to witness the final hours because they believed the dying person's fate could be decided then, dependent on whether one chose the angels that surrounded the bed or the devils. A calm death indicated the angels had triumphed. Post-Reformation Protestants insisted that one could not decide one's own fate at the last minute, a posture that must have created a certain amount of deathbed anxiety. Nonetheless, Elizabeth's Protestant chaplain was at pains to describe her last breath in terms of a direct ticket to heaven. She "departed this life, mildly," he reported, "like a lamb, easily like a ripe apple from the tree."[13]

A Christian deathbed in full flow. The demise of Reverend John Wesley. A lithograph from c. 1840.

In Islam family and friends would likewise gather around the deathbed. As the end approached they would encourage the dying person to profess her or his faith with the Arabic prayer "There is no god but God, and Mohammed is his messenger." In the original the prayer is rather comfortingly lyrical with repeated "la" sounds. If the soon-to-be-defunct was too unwell the sacred words would be whispered into the ear, just as they had been whispered to the child at birth. After death the body would be ritually washed, shrouded, and then placed in a coffin usually laid upon a bier. The burial would happen as soon as possible, ideally within a day, followed by a mourning period. Hygiene and impending rot were no doubt the driver behind this speed, for cremation is forbidden in Islam. Such had long been the case in Judaism too.

European Jews of the sixteenth and seventeenth centuries considered it a mitzvah, a good deed or religious duty, to surround the deathbed. The community did its utmost to ensure that no one died alone. Ideally, the dying person would offer a confession before ten Jews, which involved reciting a set prayer, after which the dying person would offer blessings or prayers to his or her family. Following death, the body had to be cleaned and buried within twenty-four hours. In a Talmudic passage God says, "I had placed my image among you, and for your sins I upset it; upset now your beds."[14] To honor this, mourning Jews traditionally overturned their couches or beds and left them on the floor for the seven days of shivah.

Seventeenth-century Europeans described similar scenes of funerary support along the African Gold Coast. Though no European was intimate enough with any West African to fully observe a deathbed, they recalled big gatherings after death, recounting scornfully how the priest would directly address the dead person, asking him how he had died and if anyone had caused his death. In fact these are the kinds of questions most of us have, so perhaps their rituals were good for the relatives' mental health. The eldest son would then typically bury his father under or near his bed. Every morning he would ritually offer his father the first mouthful of anything he ate or drank. English colonialists called this practice barbaric and put a stop to it.

LAST WORDS

Deathbed crowds frequently leaned in toward the dying person, keen to hear her last words. Would the person sum up her life's work and purpose in one last, immortal statement? Would she become some sort of divine guide to the next world? "Bertie," croaked Queen Victoria. "I'm bored with it all," said Churchill. "I'm going to bed," barked Stalin before sending his soldiers home. "I will not be calling you anymore. You can go to bed, too." It's hard to be profound—or perhaps it is hard to care about being profound—when you are about to die.

Westerners are particularly interested in last words, a trend that goes back to the show-stopping death of Socrates, who was condemned to drink hemlock in 399 BC after he was found guilty of acting irreverently toward the gods and being a corrupting influence on Athenian youth. His young disciple Plato recorded the unfolding events, which culminated in Socrates's drinking the poison, lying down (presumably on a bed), covering himself with a sheet, and letting the toxin slowly work its way up his body from feet to head. At the last moment he apparently removed the cloth from his face to remind a friend attending the death, "Crito, I owe a cock to Asclepius [the god of medicine]; will you remember to pay it?"[15]

What an anticlimax, we might think. But his friends were awestruck: Socrates was virtuous to the end. To the Romans, the Socratic Death was the ultimate passing, and so began the fashion of paying special attention to a person's last words. The Roman philosopher Seneca decided to kill himself in a manner similar to Socrates's and made sure his secretary was present to record his last words. "Being forbidden," he said, according to Tacitus, "to show gratitude for your services, I leave you my one remaining possession, and my best: the pattern of my life. If you remember it, your devoted friendship will be rewarded by a name for virtuous accomplishments."[16] Others claim he managed one libation for Jupiter the Liberator. That is probably more likely since, as Tacitus tells us, Seneca's death was botched, messy, and lengthy. Death by hemlock usually causes violent convulsions, cramps, and vomiting. Far tidier to go with crucifixion, which even in Greek times was a common way of killing convicts.

Given the issues with hemlock, it is quite likely that Socrates's last words as well as his demeanor were also an invention. All of the best last lines probably were. The first emperor Augustus allegedly said, "I found Rome a city of clay but left it a city of marble," though his wife Livia, equally dubiously, claimed he actually quoted a few apt lines from a Greek play. Elizabeth I, probably fictitiously, said, "All my possessions for a moment of time." Oscar Wilde, who died penniless in a Paris rooming house, is widely quoted as saying, "Either this wallpaper goes, or I do," but in reality he said these words weeks before his death.

Since the dead can't answer back, it's easy to invent their last words. Jesuits and other North American missionaries often recounted dying speeches of the native "Indians," which they used to further their cause. Their model Indian deathbed scene tended to begin with the realization that the end was near. If already a Christian convert, the Indian would pray for God, for the health of friends and family, for mercy, or for the missionaries' continued success in converting non-Christian Indians. The last words always tended to be something appropriate like "Jesus, take me!," spoken with eyes fixed longingly toward the sky.

Occasionally a person about to die but otherwise in good health can say something remarkable, as when George Engel shouted from the gallows in 1887, "Hurrah for anarchy! This is the happiest moment of my life!" Written "last words" also allow more thought. Tweets and social media are the current favorite. Leonard Nimoy, *Star Trek*'s Spock, sent as his final tweet, "A life is like a garden. Perfect moments can be had, but not preserved, except in memory. LLAP [live long and prosper]."[17] The final tweet can, however, be unexpected, as in the case of Reeva Steenkamp, who wrote, "What do you have up your sleeve for your love tomorrow??? #get excited

#Valentines Day."[18] She did not know that her lover, the Olympic sprinter Oscar Pistorius, was about to shoot her.

YOUR OWN DEATHBED

Thomas Hardy wrote of Tess d'Urberville, "There was another date . . . that of her own death; a day which lay sly and unseen among all the other days of the year, giving no sign or sound when she annually passed over it; but not the less surely there."[19] The Bible tells us that date will usually come after three score years and ten. A wisdom text from the Syrian city of Emar had the gods allotting man a maximum lifetime of 120 years and defines seeing the fourth generation of your family as the ultimate blessing of being in your nineties, the decade it defines as extreme old age.

You and I know we're going to die. According to the Greek philosopher Epicurus, this knowing does more to get in the way of our happiness than almost anything else. He urged his followers to embrace death and enjoy life, remarking that there was nothing to fear in death, which was without sensation, or in God. Yet how many heed his advice? We in the modern West tend to fight death or else ignore it. Our attitude toward the deathbed says it all. Formerly a public place, it is now hidden behind hospital curtains or gone altogether. Many of us would rather cross the street than talk to a bereaved person, whether because we are unversed in dealing with death or because we wish to deny its existence.

There's even a movement in North America that believes if we commit to enough positive thinking we can live forever. Companies such as Arizona-based Alcor offer cryonic preservation: the option to freeze your body after death so that you can be revived when future technology makes this possible. Death is simply not acceptable. We even fight to prolong the life of those with no seeming quality of life. In three high-profile cases in the United Kingdom during the late 2010s, parents campaigned to keep alive extremely sick comatose babies against the advice of their doctors. Each effort drew massive public support; in one case Donald Trump even petitioned the pope.

We look very far back in history to see how profoundly things have changed. In nineteenth-century Europe and North America it was quite common to lose at least one child, and, as we have seen, a woman might have a one-in-seven chance of dying herself in her childbearing years. This didn't necessarily make death easier. Witness Queen Victoria's forty-year mourning for her beloved Prince Albert and the Mesopotamian belief that a stillborn child would play forever in heaven, a notion clearly intended to comfort grieving parents. Death was ubiquitous and public. It had to be borne, if not accepted, and its pain shared. People gathered around deathbeds because death was an ever-present part of life.

The British government's online listing of the state photograph of the dead Victoria on her bed describes it as "rather shocking." Her eyes shut, the dead queen lies on a bed swathed in white fabric and adorned with flowers, portraits of her husband hanging above her head. The photograph and the associated airbrushed postmortem painting look thoroughly mawkish to modern eyes. Yet in Victoria's day neither her postmortem photo nor her portrait were considered at all shocking. It had long been the European fashion to commission a painting of the family grouped around the deathbed when a wife died. Such staged deathbed portraiture is now considered deviant. The last artistic Western photos of anyone on his or her deathbed are probably those of Andy Warhol's superstar, the transsexual Candy Darling, who died of lymphoma in 1974. In full Marilyn Monroe makeup, she raises her young arms seductively over her head and lies back on a white-sheeted bed surrounded by flowers. It remains a controversial image, perhaps more so the further we move from the Victorian era.

Queen Victoria took things to extremes even by the standards of her day: she wore black after Albert's death not for the conventional one year but for forty. She kept his bedchamber forever untouched after death: the glass from which he took his last sip remained on his bedside table, his blotting book and pen remained open at its last entry, and she ordered fresh flowers to be delivered to his room daily. This was not seen as disturbing or unbalanced behavior: people commended her devotion.

Regular communication with the dead, however—whether Victoria ritually sending flowers to Bertie's bedside or the precolonial West African son offering his dead father the first bite of food—challenges us. These behaviors strike us as indulgent, distasteful, sometimes utterly repugnant, as, for example, when we turn to the people of the Torajo area of modern Indonesia. There we find groups who practice traditional animism, mixed with some Islam and Christianity. These families push our modern Western death taboo to the limits: they keep their dead relatives in the house, sometimes for years, until they can afford a suitably lavish funeral. The slowly desiccating corpse is placed in an open coffin on a bed in the front room and is cared for as though it were sick rather than deceased, with food, cigarettes, and coffee given each day. After burial the bodies are still not left alone but are dug up every three years in a special ceremony in which the corpse is washed and redressed. To the Torajans, this behavior is normal and comforting.[20]

Yet many of us in the modern West have never seen a dead body, and the thought of seeing one is abhorrent. The 2016 video of David Bowie's last song, "Lazarus," shows the dying singer on a hospital bed reaching up for the camera. The film is seen as being in horrifically bad taste, which may explain why the director subsequently claimed that the video "had nothing to do with him being ill," emphasizing that his illness was shown to be terminal only after the video was shot. The deathbed now generally appears only in fiction.

Some of the best and worst horror movies involve deathbeds. Given that the deathbed is now taboo in polite society, such movies are invariably regarded as X-rated, lowbrow, deviant, or all three. Films featuring deathbeds range from *The Exorcist* (1973), called the "scariest horror movie of all time"—in which the worst scenes feature a vomiting, devil-infested, head-turning girl on a bed—to movies about killer beds themselves. Among them is the low-budget film *Death Bed: The Bed That Eats* (1977), in which a demon creates a bed to ravish a woman he loves. Then, featuring an under-bed killer monster, there's *Under the Bed* (2012), which was such an underground hit that it was followed by *Under the Bed 2* and *3*. *Sleep Tight* (2011) and *Death Bed* (2002) likewise tap into our fears about death, sleep, and beds.

How we scare ourselves! We have come far in our fight against death. The hospital bed, with its sanitized sheets and isolating curtains, is where lives are saved. It is also where 50 percent of us will die, though many surely wish they could do it somewhere else. Perhaps it would be cathartic and helpful to bring back the tradition of gathering a crowd around the deathbed to say our last goodbyes and hand out forgiveness. Then let's lay the dead body on a bed for all to see and accept and hold a funeral involving loud drums, the beating of breasts, the support of friends, and a big feast. Humans are, above all, sociable creatures.

SIX

Strange Bedfellows

Prince Ludwig of Anhalt-Köthen, a principality in central Germany, was an unremarkable traveler through England whose only distinction was that he kept his diary in execrable poetry. In 1596 he stayed at the White Hart Inn in the small town of Ware in Hertfordshire, north of London. Ware was a major stopping point for medieval pilgrims and travelers, and local hostelries competed furiously for their business. To draw adventurous tourists, the owners of one of them, probably the White Hart itself, had the brilliant idea of commissioning a massive four-poster called the Great Bed, which they publicized as fit for twelve travelers. Prince Ludwig marveled at the Great Bed's dimensions and was the first visitor to leave a record of what soon became a popular place to spend the night: "Four couples might cozily lie side by side / and thus without touching each other abide."[1]

The Great Bed, designed around 1590 by the Dutch architect, painter, engineer, and garden designer Hans Vredeman de Vries, is around twice the size of a modern double bed, measuring over

The Great Bed of Ware, exhibited in the Victoria and Albert Museum, London.

3 meters both long and wide and 2.5 meters high and weighing about 640 kilograms. Local craftsmen fabricated it from oak in forty parts, with huge bedposts made by gluing several pieces of wood together. They carved the bed with intricate European Renaissance patterns arranged in marquetry panels that were originally brightly painted, though few traces of color remain. The bed, once it was finished, was soon popular with visitors, both the curious and what one writer charmingly called "the coital," some of whom carved their initials in the wood or left red seal impressions on the bedposts.

Such was the bed's fame that it appears in Shakespeare's *Twelfth Night* (1602). There, Sir Toby Belch tells Sir Andrew Aguecheek to compose a challenge for a duel with Duke Orsino's serving boy Cesario, but the letter would be replete with falsehoods: "As many lies as will lie in thy sheet of paper, although the sheet were big enough for the bed of Ware in England."[2] Three years later a rollicking Jacobean play entitled *Northward Ho* ends with "Come, we'll dare our wives to combat in th' great bed in Ware." Ben Jonson referred to the bed in his 1609 play *The Silent Woman*. And a century later George Farquhar referred to a bed in *The Recruiting Officer* (1706) as "bigger by half than the Great Bed of Ware." The literary allusions have continued into modern times, as in a 2001 poem by Andrew Motion that has the Great Bed "shaking its sleepers out like a leaf-squall."[3]

Some of the visitors to the bed were clearly there for a prank. The *London Chronicle* for July 4, 1765, recounts (no doubt apocryphally) that twenty-six butchers and their wives—a total of fifty-two people—spent a night in the bed in 1689. Ware's pride and joy became a metaphor for needless public extravagance. In 1856 the newly consecrated and apparently rather self-important bishop of Bristol occupied a carved, canopied pew that looked like a four-poster bed, drawing ironic comparisons to the Great Bed of Ware.

As an enduring curiosity the Great Bed passed around Ware from inn to inn until the late nineteenth century, when it became a fixture in nearby Hoddeston, a popular weekend destination for railway travelers. It almost went to the United States in 1931, but the Victoria and Albert Museum in London acquired it for £4000 instead. This was a successful acquisition, for the bed is among the museum's most popular exhibits. It has remained there ever since, except for a year's visit to the small museum in Ware in 2012, financed by the UK's Lottery Commission at a cost of £229,200 (about $300,000). The curators needed six days to dismantle the bed and nine more to move it to Ware.

The last known person to occupy the Great Bed was the actress Elizabeth Hurley, who, in 2015, overstepped a guardrail to strike "saucy" poses on it during a cocktail party at the Victoria and Albert

Museum. The alarms promptly went off, and Hurley was escorted out. The British tabloids went crazy. The subtext, of course, was that a bed designed for so many can mean only one thing. Yet while some past sleepers acknowledged its erotic possibilities, many did not. Sharing a bed for platonic social sleeping was once perfectly normal. Almost every possible group slept together at some point in the past: families, friends, masters and servants, and complete strangers. Sex sometimes came into it, but often the arrangement was the product of practical considerations: the cost of beds, the need to keep warm in a world before electricity, and the sense of security bedmates provided.

TRAVELING BEDFELLOWS

The Great Bed of Ware was famous because of its size—a big bed was a sign of wealth and luxury—not because of the act of sleeping with strangers. Travelers overnighting at an inn would often share beds with unknown others. Social sleeping was popular and remains so in Asia and elsewhere, especially in rural Mongolia.

In China and Mongolia *kangs*, or mat-covered heated masonry platforms, were common in roadside inns into the twentieth century. The earliest forms, which appear around 5000 BC, were clay floors heated by fires that were swept away before sleeping. More elaborate kangs came into use as early as the fourth century BC. These were heated by cooking fires in an adjacent room or by a stove set below the floor. A typical kang could take up half to a third of a room and maintain its heat throughout the night. They were used not only for sleeping but also for eating and socializing. Eventually, many of them acquired rails, and sometimes the elite slept separately.

Today, the only time a Western traveler might routinely sleep next to a stranger is on an overnight flight. There are unspoken rules of etiquette, such as keeping to your side of the armrest, not touching, and being quiet. These rules are not much different from those laid out in a medieval French phrase book compiled for English travelers, which includes translations for "you pull all the bed clothes," "you do nothing but kick about," and "you are an ill bedfellow."[4] As in the case of ancient kangs or modern airlines, the quality of your night's sleep depended on your wealth. In poorer inns the supposed bed might be a simple wooden bench with a rope hung horizontally at chest height. Guests would sit crammed together on the bench, hang their arms over the rope, and slump over to sleep. During popular events like pilgrimages space was often in demand—again, the wealthy had the advantage. A rich person who could pay could have you kicked out of bed. It didn't matter how wise, holy, sick, or pregnant you might be. Mary and Joseph were famously stuck in an inn's stable with their baby, to be joined by a flow of visitors who presumably also had to sleep there.

Christian art illustrates the chasm between our views of bed sharing and those of earlier times. This gap is especially clear in the images of the Magi, the three wise men from the East who came with gifts for Jesus. According to Saint Matthew, they had a dream in which God warned them not to trust Herod, and the Dream of the Magi was a favorite image in art of the later Middle Ages. In such pictures the three are always shown tucked in bed together, sometimes naked but always wearing their crowns.

There was nothing sexual about these journeying men sleeping together. In *Moby-Dick*, published in 1851, Herman Melville describes how Ishmael, a young mariner, is told he must share his hostel bed with a "head harpooneer." "There's plenty room for two to kick about in that bed; it's an almighty big bed that," the innkeeper reassures him. But as Ishmael awaits the harpooner's arrival he cannot sleep, complaining that his mattress must be stuffed with corncobs or maybe broken crockery. Finally, the man, Queequeg, arrives: "Good heavens! What a sight! Such a face! . . . Yes, it's just as I thought, he's a terrible bedfellow; he's been in a fight." Nonetheless his bed partner puts out his pipe when requested to do so and "[rolls] over to one side as much as to say—'I won't touch a leg of ye.'" Finally Ishmael drifts off, awakening the next morning to find Queequeg's arms wrapped around him and having "never slept better in my life."[5]

When judges and lawyers traveled the circuit of courthouses with Abraham Lincoln they often slept two in a bed and eight in a room. Some commentators, noting how for some years Lincoln shared his permanent bed with Joshua Speed, take this to mean he was gay. Others suggest he simply enjoyed a close platonic relationship with Speed at a time when such sleeping arrangements were "allowed." Whatever his true sexuality, it is unlikely that Lincoln was engaging in eight-way orgies every night. Nonsexual bed sharing among travelers was part of everyday life in the past. In the early twentieth century, when the boardinghouse of the novelist Thomas Wolfe's mother in North Carolina filled up early in the evening, traveling salesmen would routinely sleep two to a single bed.

These arrangements didn't always go well. In his autobiography John Adams recounts how he spent a disastrous night while on the road with Benjamin Franklin. It was September 1776, shortly after the thirteen American colonies had declared independence from Britain, and the two men were members of a delegation sent by the Continental Congress to negotiate a possible end to the Revolutionary War. En route they stopped for the night at a New Jersey inn. Since they couldn't each get a room they had to share a bed "in a chamber little larger than the bed, without a Chimney, and with only one small Window."[6] This "one small window" was the cause of their consternation. Adams, who was "an invalid and afraid of the air in the night," immediately shut it. Franklin, who wanted it open, lectured Adams on his "theory of colds" and how he would suffocate without fresh air. Ultimately Adams won the battle of the window, but the peace conference was a failure.

A FAMILY AFFAIR

Jean Liedloff, famous for her best-selling 1975 book on child rearing *The Continuum Concept: In Search of Happiness Lost*, acquired an early fascination with Tarzan, jungles, and, later, Amazonian child care. She visited South America five times and lived with the Yequana Indians of the Venezuelan rain forest. Although she detailed many aspects of their lives, the only information she offered about adult sleeping customs came in one parenthetical statement: the Yequana, she wrote, "[had a] habit of telling a joke in the middle of the night, when everyone was asleep. Though some were snoring loudly, all would awaken instantly, laugh and in seconds resume sleep, snoring and all. They did not feel that being awake was more unpleasant than being asleep, and they awoke fully alert, as when a distant pack of wild boar[s] was heard by all the Indians simultaneously, though they had been asleep, while I, awake and listening to the sounds of the surrounding jungle, had noticed nothing."[7] In the jungle, in the open, in the cold, or in places and eras without lamplight or electricity, sleeping with your brethren was an eminently practical way of gaining both security and warmth.

The anthropologist John Whiting observed in the 1960s that mothers bedded with their infants in two-thirds of the societies he assessed, though the sleeping practices varied considerably. In slum areas of India whole families might sleep on the floor of the same room. Among the Nso farmers of West Cameroon, a mother would sleep in a bed with all of her children lined up behind her, the youngest closest to her, and she would always face the door to protect the children from bad spirits that might harm them or wish to take them back. The father had his own bed elsewhere.[8] Whiting also found a commonsense correlation between climate and bed partners. Separate beds featured more often in warmer environments, as among the indigenous Amazonians who sleep in individual hammocks, while whole families often shared beds in regions where the winter temperatures fall below ten degrees Celsius.

Where a living space had no dividing walls—for example, in Europe's Bronze Age round houses or Iron Age long houses—the group would inevitably sleep together. The same applies today among those living in wall-free tents or yurts, such as the nomadic pastoralists who range across Mongolia, Tibet, Central Asia, Iran, Turkey, northeastern and western Africa, and the Arabian Peninsula.[9] Maintaining elements of a lifestyle first practiced by the Scythians around 800 BC, they move with their flocks, pitching their tents along the way. Their beds vary, but most favor woven floor coverings and mats rather than furniture per se. Easy to transport and to store when out of use, the mats are laid out in a row or strewn across the floor when in use. Only for newlyweds might a pseudowall be set up, perhaps by hanging a curtain along a cord to provide some privacy, but once the first child is born the couple joins the rest of the family to sleep together: grandparents with grandchildren, fathers with children, mothers with babies.

A premodern Italian proverb advised sleepers, "In a narrow bed, get thee in the middle." The English had a phrase, "to pig," meaning to sleep with one or more bedfellows, while a "bed-faggot" was the eastern English name given to an unruly bedfellow, faggots being a traditional regional dish of fatty, roughish lumps of rolled meat cooked in gravy. As in Whiting's study of aboriginal peoples, large European families often assigned spots in the bed according to age and sex. Daughters might sleep next to their mother, sons by the father, and the oldest daughter against the wall furthest from the door. Visitors and strangers lay at the edges. Everyone shared the bedding, although pillows were considered effeminate. A sixteenth-century commentator remarked that a man should be content with a "good round log" as a pillow. Poorer folk simply hit the hay, literally bedding down together on the floor, which they would cover with straw before laying down their blankets.

Within the medieval manor house, staff would typically sleep together in the great hall, with perhaps only the lord and lady retreating to their own chamber. Most servants slept on simple pallet beds, essentially wooden boxes, sometimes on low legs, that could easily be moved from room to room. Members of the household, servants, and visitors could use such beds as and when required. Servants, brothers, sisters, and visitors would routinely sleep in the same room in or beside the same bed. These flexible arrangements continued into the eighteenth century, inventories from the time listing not only truckle beds but also "buror bedsteads that fitted under desks," "turn up bedsteads," "desk beds," and a "chest of drawers bedstead."[10] In his 1756 book on architecture Isaac Ware wrote that it was both convenient and practical for London houses to contain temporary bedsteads that could be assembled wherever visitors were to be accommodated.

PILLOW TALK

The leveling and vulnerable nature of sleep and the dark meant that bed sharing offered an opportunity to transgress social norms.[11] The hierarchical relationship between a master or mistress and their servants could loosen. In his 1836 tell-all *The Life and Confession of Isaac Heller*, the troubled author, who was later hanged for murdering his family with an axe in Liberty, New York, relates how he was sometimes so scared of the night that he'd seek comfort by sleeping alongside the "black persons" who worked on his farm. In a patriarchal society, women might use the night to express themselves, as John Eliot of Connecticut complains in his 1768 diary. Recalling the bedtime onslaughts of his wife's so-called curtain lectures, he describes how she kept both of them up through the night with her "raking up the old stories about the first & second wife, first & second children etc."[12]

Bed sharing also allowed otherwise forbidden sexual relationships, including between unmarried servants, same-sex individuals, and masters and servants. Mistresses would sometimes share their beds with female servants to protect them from the unwanted advances of male members of the household. Servants often slept at the foot of their masters' beds, no matter what was happening elsewhere in the bed. The New Englander Abigail Willey of the 1600s would put her children in the center if she was not in the mood for sex.

Yet the night can bring deep bonds of intimacy too. In some European communities unmarried youngsters of the opposite sex were allowed to bed together to judge potential compatibility. In this practice, called bundling, a partition known as a bundling board would be put down the center of the bed and absolutely no sex was allowed. It is still practiced by ultraconservative groups like the Swartzentruber Amish, who allow the couple to bundle but require them to remain fully clothed, engage in no touching, and talk all night.

Bed sharing can bring connection and the fun of freewheeling conversation after dark. Samuel Pepys was a great fan of sleeping with others—not only women but also his platonic friends. In his seventeenth-century diary, whose entries often famously ended with the words "and so to bed," he ranked his bedfellows according to their conversation skills and behavior in bed. Among his favorite bedmates were the merchant Thomas Hill, who could talk about "most things of a man's life"; John Brisbane, "a good scholar and sober man"; and "merry" Mr. Creed, who provided "excellent company."[13]

Co-sleeping is still commonplace in many societies. The Japanese call it *soine*, and they value the warm, cozy physical experience and feelings of security (*anshinkan*) it provides.[14] *Soine* is especially

Girls in Bed Room. Two Japanese girls sleeping on a mat, a photograph by Kusakabe Kimbei.

common in families with young children. *Anshinkan* is best described as safe intimacy and refers in particular to infants sleeping between their parents. Sight, gaze, recognizing familiar faces—all these add to infants' security and better sleep. Co-sleeping infants touch, suckle, and breathe with their caregivers in a kind of mutual mingling that lasts even after everyone has woken up.

The futon is considered better for *soine* than a conventional bed higher off the floor. It offers several advantages: more space to sleep as the child grows older, more comfort, and the ease of adding to it as the family grows. The futon enables flexible togetherness and warmth, while conventional double beds have boundaries and are designed for exclusive relationships. Futons are folded up during the day and can be laid anywhere, eliminating the need for separate rooms for different family members or guests. Soine is an idea of interdependence that extends far beyond the bed or futon. Kusakabe Kimbei's photograph "Girls in Bed Room," from about 1880, shows two Japanese girls, who may or may not be related, sleeping together on their mat bed with its embroidered coverlet. A book lies by the side of the bed, and painted screens hang all around. The two girls lie facing the camera, eyes shut, blissfully content in each other's company.

SLEEPING WITH BABY

Sleeping with infants, however, could be a whole other, even tragic, matter. "When the childe was a-sleepe / At night, I suck'd the breath," says a witch in Ben Jonson's 1609 *The Masque of Queenes*.[15] Sudden Infant Death Syndrome, or SIDS (previously known as Cot Death), is the name we give to the still largely unexplained bed deaths of children under a year old, most fatalities happening between midnight and 9:00 a.m. In the past, overlaying, in which a sleeping parent suffocates the child, was the main reason given for these deaths. A passage in the Old Testament says "This woman's child died in the night; because she overlaid it." The ancient Greek physician Soranos of Ephesus said that to avoid the suffocation of babies they should not share a bed with their carers but be placed in a crib alongside the bed of the mother or wet nurse.[16] In reality, there are probably many factors involved in SIDS, including infections, genetic disorders, exposure to tobacco smoke, and suffocation after becoming entangled in bedding—though placing the baby on its back has been shown to reduce rates of death. Yet in our attempt to protect against the horror of SIDS, the bed has been cast as either the biggest demon or the greatest savior, depending on one's position on bed sharing.

The American Academy of Pediatrics recommends "room-sharing without bed-sharing," stating that bed sharing increases the risk of

SIDS by 50 percent. The National Health Service in the United Kingdom reports a fivefold increase in the risk of SIDS associated with bed sharing in breast-fed babies who were under three months old, had parents who did not smoke, and whose mother had not had any alcohol or drugs. The official message is clear: bed sharing can kill your child.[17]

Contrast this with research by the biological anthropologist James McKenna, who has investigated mother–child co-sleeping and believes it is not only safe but also a "biological imperative" that leads to better child and maternal health. He draws on three epidemiological studies that show how co-sleeping reduces an infant's chances of dying by half.[18] Most of the non-Western world today agrees that the mother's bed is the best place for a new baby: it allows comfort and easy feeding, and, as Pepys knew, sleeping together tightens the bonds of affection. Yet non-Western mothers who co-sleep with their babies also have a higher child mortality rate. Is this a reason not to do it? The pro-co-sleepers argue that the higher rates are probably related to poverty rather than to bed sharing per se. The only fair comparison, they say, is with Japan, which is wealthy and highly industrialized and has almost universal infant co-sleeping with parents, often until the age of ten for boys. It also has one of the lowest infant mortality rates in the world.

As the bed debate rumbles on, the babies sleep—a lot. Bed sharing notwithstanding, throughout history we find beds just for babies: hammocks, hanging cradles, baskets, and cribs. These could be moved near to the caregivers to accommodate napping children during the day. In AD 79, when Vesuvius stubbed out life at the wealthy Roman seaside town of Herculaneum, a baby was left behind in one such cradle. Found in the living room of a house in the quarter called Insula Orientalis I, the birdlike skeleton lay on a mattress that seems to have been stuffed with foliage. European manuscripts reveal an upsurge in illustrations of rocking cradles in the thirteenth century. The infants tend to be shown swaddled in cloth bands, arms by their sides, and sometimes tied into the cradle. This binding served the dual role of protecting against rickets (or so people thought) and preventing crying. With an outstretched foot a family member could easily rock the cradle while working on something else. Upper-class families sometimes even employed rockers, nurses dedicated to cradle rocking.[19]

Royal babies often had two cradles, one for daytime and a smaller one for the night, both often decorated with gold, silver, and rich textiles. Most cradles had solid sides, perhaps with small hoods or roofs over which blankets or curtains could be draped, excellent for keeping in the warmth and keeping out any nasty fresh air. Slots on the sides of the cradles allowed them to be carried from room to room.

By the end of the eighteenth century swaddling and rocking were going out of fashion, as ideas about free movement of limbs and fresh air gained favor. Come the start of the nineteenth century, the stationary crib (or cot, as it is called in the United Kingdom) began to replace the cradle, particularly among better-off families. They had high sides with slats or spindles often made of painted metal. One side could often be slid down to allow the child to be easily picked up from its little sleeping cage. Cribs dovetailed with the new fashion of segregating one's infants in the nursery for much of the day—and all of the night. Though middle-class Victorian children no longer slept with their parents, they did continue to sleep with one another. Nonetheless, a new morality dictated that older children sleep only with same-sex siblings, which meant that even small houses were expected to have three bedrooms: one for the parents, one for girls, and one for boys.

In historical time this separation is very modern, as even in eighteenth-century England most rooms had overlapping functions that changed with the time of day. Although we sometimes find ancient beds enclosed in curtains or canopies, this was not necessarily linked to privacy or a wish to fend off potential bedfellows; instead, such canopies served other practical functions, including keeping the heat in or insects out.

The posts around the prehistoric beds at Skara Brae may have held removable canopies, in this case essential to keeping warm in the cold Scottish winter. Meanwhile, the lavishly decorated bed found in the tomb of the Egyptian queen Hetepheres 1, which dates to roughly 2580–2575 BC, was surrounded by a massive canopy, this time designed to protect against mosquitoes. The canopy was made from a collapsible rectangular framework of gilded-wood poles that would once have held a piece of fine linen that served as mosquito netting. When not in use, the curtains were stored in a box covered with semiprecious stones.

Centuries later an illustration after Gu Kaizhi (c. AD 344–406) shows a courtly Chinese canopy bed: a platform with four posts supporting fabric that might have been used to keep out insects. Like the Egyptian example, it surrounds the bed as though creating a room within a room. In China, beds were sometimes portable enough to be taken out of doors. In such cases the canopy allowed one to show off one's silks, and also protected any bedfellows from the sun. A poem from the Han Dynasty (206–20 AD) reads, "Your curtain is flapping before the bed! / I strung you to screen us from daylight. / When I left my father's house I took you with me. / Now I take you back. / I will fold you neatly and lay you flat in your box. / Curtain, will I ever take you out again?"[20]

BEDBUGS AND OTHER CREATURES

Curtained beds, sometimes built into the walls, could serve an additional purpose: they allowed animals to share the room. As long as humans have lived in houses, they have shared their space with their animals, but we do not always consider the implications. A visitor to the Hebrides in the 1780s claimed that although the urine from cows was regularly collected from the houses, the dung was removed just once a year. Pet dogs have been around royal courts since ancient times and are still in residence today. Medieval knights lie in effigy in cathedrals with a faithful hound at their feet. The thirteenth-century French king Louis XI, an amiable monarch, owned a favored greyhound named Mistodin that had not only its own bed but also special nightclothes to prevent him from catching colds. During the seventeenth century King James I of England was obsessed with hounds, and his successor Charles II was famous for his spaniels. Today, Queen Elizabeth II has her famous corgies, which reside not on her bed but in a special Corgi Room at Buckingham Palace.

Eighteenth-century Versailles teemed with dogs. The hunting dogs were kenneled outside, but most of the others slept with their masters or on their own special cushions. The Empress Josephine, Napoleon's first wife, was never far from her dogs at night. They slept on cashmere shawls or on expensive carpets. Rose petals were strewn about the bed to mask the unpleasant smells from their droppings.

People in the past had different ideas about cleanliness. Muslims were expected to undertake regular ritual ablutions with free-flowing water, as opposed to washing in still baths, which were considered dirty. Upper-class westerners, by contrast, seldom washed at all before the end of the seventeenth century. Children of the elite might not have a bath until the age of two or three. Records for Louis XIII, who was born in 1601, report that, adhering to a special royal schedule carefully devised and approved by his doctor, he took his first bath shortly before his seventh birthday. Bodily fluids were thought to be protective, and too much water was regarded as injurious.

Yet around the fifteenth century some European critics began to condemn communal sleeping on hygienic and moral grounds. Lice were perhaps the most feared animal bedfellow, for they carried a heavy social stigma. They were a common but difficult problem, and the only way to get rid of them was by regularly combing and washing one's hair and beard. Fine-tooth combs designed to trap and remove eggs and lice were an essential personal item. When archaeologists excavated a sunken Tudor warship, the *Mary Rose*, they found that nearly every drowned sailor carried a comb.

Cimex lectularius, the common bedbug, lives on human blood.[21] Its taxonomic name, coined by Carl Linnaeus, means "bug of the bed." Bedbugs may have originated as bat parasites in Middle Eastern caves, changing their host species when people began camping there. Fossilized bedbugs date to before 3500 BC, but they came into their own with the growth of cities and their densely packed populations. They have been found at El-Amarna, the pharaoh Akhenaten's capital downstream from Thebes, dating to the fourteenth century BC; and they plagued Greeks as early as 400 BC. Chinese writers complained about bedbugs as early as the eighth century AD.

Myths proliferated. Pliny the Elder's *Natural History*, published around AD 77, argued that bedbugs had medicinal uses, a belief that persisted for centuries. As recently as the eighteenth century the French physician Jean-Étienne Guettard recommended that they be used to treat hysteria. Linnaeus himself proclaimed that they could cure earaches.

Bedbugs turn out to have no medicinal uses, and their annihilation has obsessed bed owners for millennia. All kinds of poisonous and dangerous substances have been thrown at them. The usual English method of thoroughly washing cloth by bucking, or soaking in lye—a solution made from ashes and urine—did not help. Others opted to scatter their rooms with alder leaves and slices of bread smeared with glue to act as traps. An advertisement from 1746 recommended that "Oyl of Turpentine" be applied to bedsteads and places where they bred. The eighteenth-century philosopher John Locke preferred dried kidney bean leaves under the bed as a bug repellent. Fumigation, fire, smoke from peat fires, even blowtorches, also sulfur and plain hard scrubbing were some of the usually ineffective remedies in use until DDT stopped bedbugs in their tracks in 1939.

DDT, widely used in the Second World War, was so effective that generations of baby boomers grew up with no experience of bedbugs. But it was eventually found to be so lethal to animal and especially bird populations that it was banned in 1972. Within a couple of decades bedbugs were back, in force. We're back to the age-old remedies: throwing out infected mattresses, washing linen and clothes, squashing the bugs on sight. But the bedbugs endure, even in the most expensive hotels and houses. They are the sleeper's nightmare. Getting rid of them remains a foul, itchy, complicated process.

Animal bedfellows were not always bad sorts. Even today many westerners sleep with their pets, and this was probably even more common before the advent of central heating. Elizabeth Charlotte, Princess Palatine (b. 1652), wife of the Duke of Orleans (younger brother of Louis XIV of France), once remarked that only her six small puppies kept her truly warm in bed.

BEDFELLOWS NO MORE

Despite the long history of bed sharing, by the late nineteenth century it was in decline in mainstream Europe and the United States. The nineteenth-century American physician William Whitty Hall, who was given to verbose moralizing on health issues ranging from coughs to living a long life, classed co-sleeping societies as "the vilest and filthiest of the animal kingdom—wolves, hogs, and vermin." Civilized societies, he lectured readers, kept separate beds. Yet this concept of privacy remains far less important to many people outside the West. The Japanese don't even have their own word for it, instead using an adaptation of the English word, *praibashii*.

Yet in the modern West platonic co-sleeping happens only in a handful of atypical situations, such as airplanes, prison cells, camping, and long-distance yacht races; and among youngsters in boarding schools and youth hostels or at pajama parties. Even then, the bed itself is rarely shared. Occasionally a bed might have multiple sleepers—but never at the same time. Gizelle Schoch, a South African friend, told us that many of her friends had to share beds when they first arrived in London: "The city is expensive, so there was often no other option. I remember one four-bed house had nineteen guys bed sharing. They didn't sleep together though, they just used the beds in shifts."[22] The filmmaker John Herbert told us about his time in the 1990s shooting footage in the Arabian Gulf and North Sea, where people would "hot bed" on the oil rigs and supply ships. Each bunk bed would have three designated occupants every twenty-four hours, but in sequence at eight-hour intervals and never together. Submarine crews routinely hot-bunked during the Second World War. It is still commonplace when military operations make it necessary.

Other instances of forced bed sharing occur only when humans are subjected to dehumanizing and degrading behavior, as, for example, when African slaves were jammed together in the holds of colonists' boats, or in the Nazi death camps, where detainees would sleep in bunks of three or more levels, each with several occupants.

In the 2008 film *Bedfellows*, said to be the scariest two-and-a-half-minute movie ever made, a woman receives a phone call in the middle of the night and discovers that sleeping next to her is not her husband but a nightmare ghoul. This short is possibly almost as horrific as the singer Kanye West's 2016 video for *Famous*, which features twelve naked celebrity sleepers, apparently including

Kanye, Donald Trump, George W. Bush, Kim Kardashian, and Amber Rose.[23] All are lined up on a sort of modern Bed of Ware, snuffling, shuddering, and slightly damp: the result is unnerving. The message is clear: for us in the modern West the very idea of bedfellows is a nightmare.

SEVEN

The Moving Bed

Monarchs traveled much of the time. They had to project their power and be seen by their subjects in eras long before the day of royal trains, limousines, and private planes. The stakes could be high. Many people, for instance, assume that because it lasted so long as a continuous political entity, ancient Egypt was a stable, peaceful kingdom—a serene realm where the pharaohs symbolized balance between order and chaos and kept enemies at bay.

In fact, Egypt was a land of conflicting loyalties, with a court often riven with competing factions; a kingdom of provinces, towns, and villages as well as competing deities nurtured by powerful cults. The pharaoh presided over this tapestry of rival interests by a combination of carefully supervised administration, religious ideologies, and military power. These realities kept the monarch and his high officials constantly on the move. They traveled to preside over major festivals honoring the sun god Amun and other deities. Stately royal progresses carried them by boat the length of their domains. Some pharaohs, like the New Kingdom rulers Thutmose III (fifteenth century BC) and Seti I (early thirteenth century BC), were ambitious conquerors; others were content to administer the territory they inherited or were forced to defend against invaders. Whatever their preferences, all pharaohs had to appear in public before the people, far from their palaces, which meant they had to sleep away from their bedchambers. They still, however, had to slumber clear of the ground. They used folding travel beds.

TRAVELING BEDS

The tomb of the young Egyptian king Tutankhamun (late fourteenth century BC) yielded one of the earliest-known travel beds and the earliest triple-folding example.[1] Two-fold beds were used earlier, which is hardly surprising since they are much easier to make. Tutankhamun's travel bed folded in a Z shape and seems to have been made specially for him. The process appears to have been a matter of trial and error, for the artisans drilled extra holes near the hinges that were never used. Four wooden lion legs rested on copper alloy drums, attached to a timber frame with a woven mat fabricated from three linen strips. This was a carefully crafted, lightweight cot whose design the researcher Naoko Nishimoto has described as "inherently poetic."

Commoners traveled far more simply and were often little more than migrant workers. They were anonymous armies of laborers and soldiers, boatmen and stoneworkers, who worked for rations on public projects of all kinds. Some were teams from different villages, drafted to construct pyramids during the quiet agricultural months. Others may have spent their whole lives traveling from job to job, laboring obediently under harsh conditions. Only rarely can we see where and how they slept. The Pyramids of Giza near Cairo needed so many workers that a large pyramid-workers' town rose to the south of the great monuments behind a huge limestone wall ten meters high. The Egyptologist Mark Lehner uncovered an

Tutankhamun's three-part camp bed.

extensive urban site that included workshops, bakeries, and a complex of galleries that served as barracks. The Gallery Complex consisted of four blocks of sleeping platforms with colonnades of slender wooden columns that supported a light roof and fronted on the street. Each platform accommodated as many as forty or fifty laborers or guards lying packed alongside one another.[2] Presumably they slept in their clothes or else wrapped themselves in blankets. They carried few possessions, having traveled, often in teams, from their villages to the job, where basics were provided on site. The scribes and supervisors, meanwhile, lived in much more substantial housing. When the Giza project, with its thousands of people, was finished, the Pyramid Town shrank into clusters of smaller villages attached to the nearby temples.

Ancient Egyptian workers slept on the ground; millions of migrant workers and travelers around the world do so to this day.

They think nothing of it, for sleeping on the ground requires nothing more than fleeces, blankets, or one's own cape. When Telemachus, the son of the Homeric hero Odysseus, visited King Menelaus's palace, he was bedded down in the portico: "And Helen briskly told her serving women to make beds in the porch's shelter, / lay down some heavy purple throws for the beds themselves, / and over them spread some blankets, thick woolly robes, / a warm covering laid on top." Odysseus himself slept on the ground in his own palace before killing Penelope's suitors: "Spreading out on the ground the raw hide of an ox, / heaping over it fleece from sheep, then Eurynome threw / a blanket over him once he had nestled down."[3]

The twentieth-century British explorer Wilfred Thesiger was an inveterate traveler with a near-mystical devotion to tradition. He spent much of his life in remote places like the Sahara's Tibesti Mountains and Arabia's legendary Empty Quarter. Thesiger always traveled light. While living among the Marsh Arabs of southern Iraq he slept on the damp ground wrapped in blankets and wraps, oblivious to the insects that swarmed around him. In the desert he felt "in harmony with the past," traveling in the space and silence as "men had travelled for untold generations across the deserts," relying on their camels and their skills. Thesiger also traveled in the mountains of Central Asia. In 1956 he met another well-known traveler, Eric Newby, and a friend, whom he invited to stay with him. Seeing the two men blowing up inflatable air beds, he tactlessly remarked, "You must be a couple of pansies."[4] Another Eurasian traveler, the American Owen Lattimore, accompanied Mongolian camel caravans during the 1920s. He marveled at the nomads' knowledge of their beasts and of the seemingly monotonous landscape's ecology. In addition to their cargo of trade goods the camels carried food and tea for the drivers. Lattimore became accustomed to breaking camp at any hour of the night, eating whatever was at hand, and sleeping "where I could lie down." For the poor, as for the intrepid traveler, one's bed was what it had been for thousands of years.[5]

Beds were (and are) cumbersome, heavy pieces of furniture, which meant that only the wealthy might have personal portable beds—whether because they were ingenious collapsible pharaonic splendors or because servants were there to do the carrying. Premodern royal households maintained large inventories of beds, including folding camp beds used for military campaigns, and others for diplomatic occasions, which were explicitly designed to be seen and admired by others. These beds folded up, but nevertheless they could be elaborate structures complete with canopies, curtains, and other appurtenances normally found on fixed beds, so signifying the user's wealth.

The celebrated Field of the Cloth of Gold was perhaps the ultimate in movable sleeping places. It was an elaborate tented camp erected south of Calais for a meeting held from June 7 to 24, 1520, between King Henry VIII of England and King Francis I of France. Within his camp Henry erected a replica of a palace with brick foundations and canvas, timber-framed walls. Each monarch tried to outshine his rival by featuring spectacular temporary structures, feasts, and jousting. The tents and their furnishings as well as the royal beds were adorned with fabrics woven with silk and gold thread (the "cloth of gold" that gave the meeting its name). The field meeting was an extravagantly choreographed diplomatic competition that pitted monarch against monarch, even down to their lavish beds.[6]

While few occasions warranted that level of regal display, many affluent people brought elaborate sleeping places with them when they traveled. The Stockport Heritage Service in northern England owns a traveling box bed dated to around 1600. It is a thing of luxury that came complete with a set of stairs to climb into the bed, two locking wig boxes, and two carved depictions of husband and wife, suggesting it was a wedding present. The owners of such a bed had no need to bed share with traveling strangers—or their parasites. The diarist John Evelyn recalled the time he slept in another person's inn bed in Le Bouveret, Switzerland, without changing the sheets since he was "heavy with pain and drowsiness," but he "shortly after pay'd dearly for my impatience, falling sick of the Small Pox."[7]

MOVING MILITARY

Ancient soldiers on the move or on the battlefield also slept on the ground. Leather tents were in common use, carried in panels on mules. The *conturbernium* held up to eight soldiers in a space about 2.96 meters square. Larger tents were provided for centurions, who used theirs as offices also. Officers had even larger shelters, carried on several mules. Life in Roman fortresses and garrisons was more closely organized. In barracks the men lived in long blocks divided into squad rooms with a centurion's suite at one end. Eight men served in a squad, with a total of eighty men sleeping in a single block on what were probably simple bunk beds. Officers lived in more comfort. Ever since the days of Julius Caesar and probably before, easily packed campaign furniture was one of the impedimenta of senior officers. Such baggage loaded down armies to ludicrous extents, so much so that the ability of eighteenth- and nineteenth-century armies to move rapidly was seriously impeded. When Gen. Sir Colin Campbell left Lucknow after the Indian Mutiny in 1858, the baggage train extended over thirty kilometers. According to William Howard Russell of the *Times*, the general's baggage included "a variety of types of bed from four poster or tent beds" and enough furniture to fill a small house. Campaigning on this grand scale was strategically dangerous, a lesson the British learned only in the highly mobile fighting of the Boer War at the very end of the nineteenth century.

An old man in Rajastan, India, relaxes on a coir-fiber charpoy, a portable bed with legs and a woven sleeping platform.

Campbell's soldiers may have slept on charpoys—from the Persian *chihar-pai*, "four-feet"—which were in use long before the Indian Mutiny. The fourteenth-century Moroccan traveler Ibn Battuta waxed eloquent about charpoy beds in India: "The beds in India are very light. A single man can carry one and every traveler should have his own bed which a slave carries about on his head. The bed consists of four conical legs on which four staves are laid; between they plait a sort of ribbon of silk or cotton. When you lie on it you need nothing else to render the bed sufficiently plastic."[8] Charpoys were also brought to Sudan by Sikh soldiers during the colonial wars of the late nineteenth century.

Unlike Indian soldiers, most European troops slept on the ground. Military camp beds survive only in rare cases. George Washington's equipment on campaign included tents, eating uten-

Modern-day museum exhibit of Napoleon's camp bed and bedroom/study at his
headquarters on the eve of the Battle of Waterloo, 1815.

sils, and folding beds. When he traveled north to military installa-
tions from his headquarters in Newburgh, New York, he used
a folding bed with a collapsible metal frame and thin mattress.
Another folding bed, preserved at his Mount Vernon estate, was
ingeniously hinged for easy transport. On the eve of the Battle of
Waterloo the Duke of Wellington and Napoleon Bonaparte slept
less than six kilometers from each other, both on couches that were
far from opulent. The Iron Duke lay on what his biographer, friend,
and fellow soldier George Robert Gleig later described as a "cur-
tainless camp-bed with its faded silk green cover."[9] Wellington
eschewed comfort and died on this very bed at Walmer Castle in
Kent in 1852. The Emperor Napoleon spent the eve of the battle
in a collapsible camp bed that could be folded along the length and
width on ingenious ball-and-socket joints. Six legs mounted on

wheels supported the frame, to which a mattress of stripped twill was attached with bronze and iron hooks. The folded bed was carried in a stout leather case. Both the emperor and high-ranking officers used these camp beds, with or without canopies. Napoleon was so fond of his that, like the duke, he died on it in exile on Saint Helena in 1821.[10]

Some military camp beds enjoyed long lives. During the Peninsula War in Spain (1808–14), Lt. J. Malcolm of the 42nd Regiment of Foot (the Black Watch) used a bed with a light, tubular metal frame and a two-part laced canvas top that folded into a trunk. His grandson, who also served in the Black Watch, slept on it during H. H. Kitchener's Egyptian campaigns of 1882. It is now in the regimental museum.

"SAVAGE" HOLIDAYS

Camping for recreation, rather than for conquest, became popular in Britain and beyond in the late nineteenth and early twentieth centuries, in part through the beliefs espoused by the Boy's Brigade, founded in 1872, and the Scout movement, established by Gen. Robert Baden-Powell in 1910. Both organizations emphasized open-air living and the relationship between developing one's personality and nature. Baden-Powell was an outdoor fanatic, to the point that even when it snowed he slept on a bed located in an open veranda attached to his house. Thanks to scouting, recreational camping became an escape from the hectic routine of the city. Stirring accounts of explorers and missionaries traveling in remote lands and setting up tents in exotic places added to the appeal. Camping offered "savage" holidays and days in the sun and wind that tanned faces and limbs. This new enthusiasm coincided with the industrialized world's nostalgic fantasy of gentle scenery, of a mellow countryside, of "the Garden of Eden before the Fall." For the first time, camp beds entered the mainstream, for Edenic nature did not mean discomfort.

The ever-well-organized Warren Miller, the editor of the magazine *Field and Stream*, wrote in his 1915 book *Camp Craft* of various types of camp bed, including the standard stretcher bed and the more elaborate camp-cot, which folded down to "a parcel 36 by 8 inches in diameter." The outfitter Abercrombie supplied modifications of the stick bed that consisted of a khaki and wool quilt, with pockets running across it for wooden rods, that could be rolled into a 2.7 kg (6 lb.) parcel. According to Miller, ladies camping with their families "will not endure much discomfort from hard browse mattresses, rope beds, and the like."[11]

People slept in blankets and their cloaks, on mats and rugs, but the most logical form of travel bedding, wherever it was laid, was and still is the sleeping bag. Today, such bags are feather-light, portable quilts that provide thermal insulation. The modern-day camping industry offers bags for every kind of temperature and weather condition, even so-called mummy bags that include an insulated hood for the sleeper's head. Add a bivouac sack as a waterproof cover, and you have everything you need for minimalist camping or hiking in the wilderness. Sophisticated technology has turned the simple sleeping bag of the 1960s into a near-tailor-made sleeping place.

No one person invented the sleeping bag. German peasants of the 1850s used linen sacks stuffed with dry leaves, hay, or straw. Nineteenth-century French mountain patrolmen carried sheepskin knapsack bags lined with wool that were rolled up and carried with shoulder straps. In 1861 the Alpine explorer Francis Fox Tuckett tested a blanket sleeping bag with a waterproof rubber bottom. Such rudimentary sleeping arrangements were little more than open-ended, person-sized bags. A Welsh entrepreneur, Pryce Pryce-Jones of the wool- and flannel-manufacturing city of Newtown, brought the sleeping bag into the international marketplace. He developed the Euklisia Rug (Greek: *eu*, "well," and *klisia*, "cot or sleeping place"), a nearly two-meter-long wool blanket with an off-center pocket at the top for an inflatable rubber pillow. Once inside, you folded the rug over yourself to keep warm.[12]

Pryce-Jones was apprenticed to a Newtown draper at the age of twelve, then took over the business, realized the potential of the mail and rail networks, and went on to publish the world's first mail order catalogues. He sold the Russian army sixty thousand Euklisias, which were used in the Russo-Turkish War at the siege of Plevna, Bulgaria, in 1877. When the city fell, the Russians canceled the rest of their order, leaving Pryce-Jones with seventeen thousand undelivered rugs. He added them to his catalogue and sold them as an inexpensive bedding solution for charities working with the poor. The bags became so popular that they were adopted by the British army and widely used by travelers in the Australian outback. Unfortunately, no original Euklisias survive, but in 2010 the British Broadcasting Corporation commissioned a replica made from the original patent, which it then donated to a museum in Pryce-Jones's hometown.

Sleeping bags had obvious appeal for Arctic and Antarctic travelers. Before skiing across Greenland in 1888, the Norwegian explorer Fridtjof Nansen and five friends lived among Laplanders and Inuit to see how they adapted to extreme cold. Their hosts slept under sealskin blankets, so Nansen sewed up a three-person sleeping bag from them. A year later the Norwegian company G. Fuglesang AS, a wadding manufacturer, marketed commercial versions of Nansen's bags. These gradually evolved into a mummy-shaped version, some with arms and legs. Captain Robert Scott's *Discovery* expedition to the Antarctic in 1902 relied on reindeer pelt sleeping suits. Putting them on was like wrestling with a python. The British polar parties relied on man hauling, which made them sweat in their clothing. Moisture formed in the sleeping bags and froze, making them hard to roll up and difficult to get into until one's body heat softened them. Scott's rival Roald Amundsen paid careful attention to traditional Inuit and Lapp practice. Like them, he and his men wore loose-fitting fur clothing, which was efficient and protective. They also relied almost completely on sled dogs for hauling and traveled safely and much faster. Today's synthetic fills do not absorb water, and they dry easily even when thoroughly soaked. Their competitor, down, weighs less and retains heat better but has to be kept dry. Sleeping bags are now near-universal as traveling beds, so much so that we forget that until the Second World War U.S. soldiers were issued only blanket rolls and a ground sheet.

Thirteen years after Pryce-Jones filed the Euklisia sleeping bag patent, the Pneumatic Mattress and Cushion Company of Reading, Massachusetts, produced the first commercial air mattress. It looked much like the air mattresses on which our neighbors lounge in their swimming pool but was originally developed as an alternative to the hair-filled mattresses used on Atlantic steamships. Air mattresses had many advantages: they were easily deflated and stowed and at least theoretically could serve as life rafts. They were also ideal for land-lubbers moving into crowded apartments in growing cities where space was limited. The Pneumatic Mattress and Cushion Company's advertisements boasted that no bugs or germs resided in air mattresses, they never needed turning, were odorless, and never got musty or damp. An easily washed cover protected the air sack. There were three sizes: one-half, three-fourths, and full size, at "$22 and Up," including air pump and slats. There was even a thirty-day trial period with a full refund if not satisfied.

The Pneumatic Mattress was not the first of its kind. As early as the sixteenth century the French upholsterer William Dejardin developed an inflatable "wind bed" made of waxed canvas. The idea was there, but the canvas bed deflated too quickly and vanished into technological oblivion. Three centuries later the American pioneer

Margaret Frink, who traveled overland with her husband from Indiana to California during the 1849 Gold Rush, wrote of a floor put over the family baggage and rations in their covered wagon: "We had an India-rubber mattress that could be filled with either air or water, making a very comfortable bed. During the day we could empty the air out, so that it took up but little room."[13]

Today, you can buy raised inflatable beds with built-in pumps, "whoosh" valves for rapid deflation, and individual controls for indoor use as well as tougher designs for harsh traveling conditions. The ultimate is probably the "hovering bed," a daydream of the Dutch designer Janjaap Ruijssenaars. You sleep on a bed floating forty centimeters above the floor. Matching sets of repelling magnets built into the bed and the floor beneath will support almost a ton in weight. But this is no travel bed. The price is stratospheric, around $30,000 in 2019.

MOVING FURNITURE

In addition to traveling, people often moved beds around the house. This was perfectly normal in the days before rooms had single, discrete purposes. The medieval pallet bed and South Asian charpoy could be put wherever they were needed. Such beds have probably been around for as long as people have slept off the ground. Most modern Pakistani households still own charpoys. They really are flexible, multipurpose pieces of furniture that support all aspects of life. Women use them for chatting with their female friends and family; as wedding beds, all decorated with flowers; as supports for giving birth; for hanging cradles containing their babies; and for drying clothes or spices. Men might use them as pulpits to address the community or as informal places ideal for conversation. Pairs of young children can easily move them about the house—out onto the veranda or up to the roof to sleep. When used for sleeping, the charpoy is usually surrounded by a mosquito net, but a particular

bed is not necessarily imbued with any sense of individual ownership. The people of Dera Ghazi Khan, a poor town in Pakistan's
Punjab, have taken the charpoy to extremes, creating supersized
versions known as *khatts*. Seating up to two dozen apiece, they are
used as meeting places: the perfect platform for friends to gather on
holidays or in the evenings to gossip.

Variations on the regular (one-person!) charpoy theme appear in
ancient Egypt, Mesopotamia, and Greece, but it is the basic Indian
variant that has endured. Light and easy to make with fibers or cotton strips, charpoys are widely used in Sudanese towns and villages
as well as throughout Asia. Many people in rural China sleep on
woven rope beds, basically a wooden frame with rope woven tightly
to form a slightly pliable but still pretty stiff platform for a sleeping
pad or blanket. Light and portable, they are often found stacked in
simple hotels. Such beds are so light and versatile they will probably never go out of fashion.

"SLEEP NETS"

One of the simplest beds, if you can call it a bed, originated in the
Americas: the hammock. This remarkable artifact arrived in Europe
with the returning Spanish conquistadors. In 1492 Columbus wrote
of the many Indians who came to his ships every day to barter
cotton and *hamacas*, "nets in which they sleep." Before this entry
into recorded history, the hammock had been in use for many centuries in Central and South America. The Spanish word *hamaca* is
borrowed from the Arawak and Taino Indian *hamaka*, a "stretch of
cloth," actually a fabric, netting, or rope sling suspended between
two fixed points. Hammocks had great advantages in the forested
landscapes of Central and South America. They were light and
highly portable, could be set up almost anywhere between two trees,
and were extremely comfortable. Best of all, they protected their occupants from biting ants, snakes, and many insect stings and from

infectious diseases. Hammocks became an enduring image of a newly discovered America. An iconic print of 1630 by the Flemish baroque engraver Theodoor Galle shows the explorer Amerigo Vespucci awakening a beautiful Native American woman, who rises in wonder from a netting hammock.

Hammocks are never durable artifacts. They are readily made and easily discarded or lost. This means we know almost nothing of their pre-Columbian history, but they are said to have arrived in the Yucatán from the Caribbean less than two centuries before the Spanish conquest. As far as we know, they did not figure prominently in Maya culture or mythology but were widespread in Amazon forests before Europeans arrived.

Before Columbus brought them back to Europe, hammocks were unknown there as traveling beds, although cotton slings were sometimes used as carriage seats. Their main use initially was at sea: they came into their own on sailing ships around 1590 and were adopted for seamen by the Royal Navy in 1597. They were ideal for use in limited spaces, swung with the movement of the ship, and were comfortable into the bargain. There was no danger of falling out of bed in heavy seas. Tightly rolled up and lashed, they could be stowed out of the way and were stacked in nets along a warship's decks to provide extra protection in battle. Even when slung close together, the hammock offered a cocoon-like sleep. Those killed in battle or who died at sea were buried in their weighted hammocks. The demands of jungle warfare caused the US Army to adopt hammocks with mosquito nets in places like Burma during the Second World War. The US Marines used hammocks in New Britain and on other wet, insect-heavy Pacific islands. They even suspended hammocks in slit trenches to avoid gunfire. Both the Americans and the Vietcong used them during the Vietnam War. Hammocks have even traveled in space. During the Apollo program the astronauts in the lunar module slept in them between moonwalks.

Nowadays, the hammock industry is enormous, especially in Central America, where hammocks appear as often in living rooms and on verandas as in bedrooms. They are often woven on looms, a major craft in the Yucatán. There is even an annual Festival of Hammocks in San Salvador every November, when artisans sell their often brilliantly colored woven swinging beds by the hundreds. Hammocks also make remarkably good beds for babies: they curve with the child's spine, self-rock the restless infant, and can be installed anywhere.

RAIL AND ROAD

We now sleep in beds in places unimaginable two centuries ago. For thousands of years travelers were often solitary or in small groups, unless armies or fleets were involved. Stagecoaches were an ordeal on bad roads, where you shared very close quarters. Stagecoach travelers like a certain Major Hanship wrote in 1815 of "vain attempts to sleep, the bumping of the head against the side panel, while your other shoulder acts as a flying buttress to a snoring farmer."[14] He complained of cramped knees, the constant braying of the coachman's horn, and the fixed stare of an "old maid" sitting across from him. Then came mass travel via railroads, which stitched together cities and towns near and far. Journeys by rail could last for days, which meant that people had to sleep on the train. At first, passengers slept on their seats, often hard benches that made no concessions to comfort. The sleeping car first appeared in America during the 1830s. Its twenty-four beds, which could be configured into coach seats during the day, were at best uncomfortable.

In the United States one name became synonymous with civilized rail travel: George Mortimer Pullman.[15] Pullman was a cabinetmaker and engineer who made his name by raising buildings in Chicago above flood levels with screw jacks. Fresh from a very uncomfortable train ride, he decided to create sleeper cars for the

Chicago and Alton Railroad Company. He hinged the lower seats and attached iron upper berths to the roof with ropes and pulleys. The new cars were not a success, so four years later Pullman designed what he called the Pioneer, wider and taller than previous cars, with rubberized springs to soften the ride. During daylight hours the Pioneer looked like a luxurious yet conventional passenger car, but when darkness fell it became a two-story hotel on wheels. A combination of folding seats and upper berths turned the carriage into a sleeper. Specially trained porters came through to install privacy partitions and sheets. The car revealed a concern for passenger comfort at a far higher level than railroad passengers had ever seen. Pullman's sleeping cars gained a huge publicity boost from Abraham Lincoln's funeral train and soon entered commercial service. By 1867 he was running almost fifty cars on three railroads. During the peak years of American railroading there were several all-Pullman trains, including the 20th Century Limited on the New York Central Railroad.

There is something inherently romantic about lying in bed in a train. Overnight journeys between London and Scotland acquired a cachet of exotic adventure among many travelers, despite being far from comfortable. On traditional British sleepers the beds are narrow and short, making them hard on tall people. If you have an expansive waist, absentmindedly turning over may land you on the floor. But they are more comfortable than the traditional French *couchettes*, in which six strangers sleep in close proximity. Sleepers are still common in many countries, especially India, where the basic Sleeper Class provides sleeping coaches without air conditioning, with three berths across the coach and two facing long ways. The most luxurious sleepers come in Business Class, where a full-sized sleeper coach has eight cabins, two for couples. Bedding is provided along with very wide sleeper berths and carpeted compartments.

Nothing in the sleeper world today rivals the Orient Express, the ultimate paragon of railroad luxury. In 1883 the Compagnie Internationale des Wagons-Lits created the Orient Express as a showpiece of luxury travel between Paris and points east, eventually reaching as far as Istanbul. The itineraries have changed considerably over the years, the operation passing into private hands as the Venice Simplon-Orient-Express in 1982, using restored carriages from the 1920s and 1930s. In the opening decades of the twenty-first century you can travel in a double cabin with a comfortable couch that becomes a bedroom with Pullman-style beds, one up, one down. A journey on this train is a trip back to the world of Agatha Christie's immortal whodunit *Murder on the Orient Express*, but (one hopes) without the plot.

The recreational vehicle (RV for short) is a logical extension of the railroad sleeper.[16] The first motor homes, which appeared in Canada and Los Angeles around 1910, were basically converted automobiles or trailers towed behind an automobile. They literally looked like small houses on trailers. The first actual RV was Pierce-Arrow's Touring Landau, which had a backseat that folded into a bed, a chamber pot toilet, and a sink that folded down from the back of the driver's seat. The driver communicated with his passengers by telephone. Auto campers became popular during subsequent decades, partly because of the growing popularity of national parks. At first, park visitors mostly camped in tents by the roadside; later, some trailers came equipped with beds as well as tents that collapsed for travel. Many people welded tin cans to their radiators to heat food. In 1967 Winnebago began mass-producing RVs that had refrigerators, kerosene stoves, and even king-sized beads. In 2019 over eight million households in the United States and Canada own RVs and vacation in them. Another 450,000 people drive around and live in their vehicles full-time.

If sleeper travel is strangely addictive, getting to sleep in an airliner is another matter. Most of us are only too familiar with cramped economy seats, inadequate legroom, and a shuffling neighbor who snores. Rather fewer have tried Emirates First Class on a giant Airbus 380, which features a double bed and personal shower. Lesser first-class (and even the occasional business class) experiences involve flat folding seats, often long enough but too narrow to accommodate your pesky elbows. Flat seats are a far cry from the onboard beds of yesteryear, when double-decker Boeing Stratocruisers and Lockheed Constellations had space for upper and lower berths with mattresses and sheets, reading lights and curtains, and sometimes even breakfast in bed. In many respects it was an effort to replicate a railroad sleeper in an era when most people who flew commercially could afford the premium fares. Not that sleeping was all that pleasant. You were above or below your fellow passengers, many of whom drank too much of the free liquor, and passengers who booked the no smoking section (if there was one) soon discovered that the air quality was the same all over the cabin. You often slept to a background of increasingly boisterous partying. The beds vanished as aircraft like the Stratocruiser gave way to sleek jetliners and the jumbo jet, where efficiency—in the form of cramming as many bodies aboard as possible—took the place of luxury.

Despite centuries of experimentation, we've not succeeded in moving far beyond sleeping on the ground or using narrow camp beds. We wrap ourselves in blankets or sleep in bags. Thanks to space age technology, our bedding dries quicker and our camp beds are lighter. But the bed, in its ultimate refinement, is really a creature of the bedchamber.

EIGHT

The Public Bedchamber

In medieval Europe virtually everyone slept on straw, perhaps wrapped in a cloak directly on the floor or on pallets of straw stuffed into sacks, covered with hides or blankets. They often huddled together for warmth, close to the hearth, in communal dwellings that were often shared with animals. You "made your bed" by stuffing a sack full of straw. More prominent members of a landowner's dwelling might sleep in side chambers that were often lean-tos against the walls of the main dwelling or set in recesses. Windows had no glass, bedchambers could be drafty, sanitation minimal. Only the most important lords had raised bedsteads, like the mythical Beowulf, king of the Danes, who slept surrounded by "many a sea-warrior crouched to his hall-rest." Everyone slept in everything except their armor.

Beowulf's people were an uncouth lot compared to the Normans, who conquered England in 1066. They preferred more comfort and built houses where lords slept in chambers that doubled as sitting rooms. These rooms were both bedrooms and audience chambers, where everyone, from nobility to common farm laborers, was received and, if appropriate, paid. These were the prototypes of the formal royal European bedchambers of later centuries.

JUSTICE FROM BED

By the twelfth century most European royal households were organized into three divisions: a chapel, the hall, and the chamber, where the ruler slept. In Britain the master chamberlain was in charge of the chamber, where he attended the king daily. Because the monarch was closely guarded, the chamber was a safe place to keep valuables, in what was then the Treasury. From this evolved the wardrobe, which was a place to store clothes and wash oneself if running water was available and which also had a privy chamber that served as the toilet, with a bucket that was emptied regularly.

By Henry III's reign (1216–72), England's principal royal palace at Westminster in London had a Painted Chamber that served as a combined audience and bedchamber. It was 24 meters long, 7.9 meters wide, and 9.4 meters high and lavishly painted with murals depicting Virtues and Vices in pairs as well as painted guardians like King Solomon, who protected the sleeping king.[1] Tragically, this remarkable room, which lay next to the still-surviving Great Hall, burned down in 1834, but its details were well recorded. Henry's profligate spending on his bedchambers and those of his queen caused unrest among his overtaxed subjects. His successor, King Edward I (1272–1307), caused the windows of his bedchamber in the Tower of London to be glazed to reduce draughts. By this time royal beds were fairly comfortable. The poet Geoffrey Chaucer served as yeoman valet to the King's Chamber at the age of twenty-four. Among other duties he made His Majesty Edward III's "fethir bed," providing "many a pillow" and plenty of soft fabric to sleep on, so the king did not have to turn over. Chaucer remained high in royal favor. As his reputation as a poet grew and he moved on to weightier duties, the king granted him a stipend of a daily gallon of wine in 1374.

Beds loomed large in domestic inventories in royal palaces and other large establishments. The finest of them were richly decorated, with royalty sleeping on fine silk bedclothes adorned with heraldic symbols and other symbolic motifs. Household documents as well as wills record that beds were among the most precious of all personal possessions. It seems inevitable that the bed became a symbol of royalty, a stage for the drama of monarchy where the ruler sat while dispensing judgment—the state bed.

The kings of France maintained a long tradition of holding court in bed. A book of justice from the reign of Louis IX (1214–70), also known as Saint Louis, declares that the royal bed should always be in a place where the king sat in judgment. Almost half a millennium later the seventeenth-century French author and physician Bernard Le Bovier de Fontenelle remarked, "The bed of justice is where justice sleeps."[2] In his day the royal bed was on a raised dais with seven steps where the king sat or lay. High officials would stand, lesser ones kneel. The hierarchy surrounding the monarchy was always visible.

The *lit de parade* was where the monarch displayed himself on formal occasions, dressed in ceremonial finery and surrounded by the elaborate hierarchy of courtiers and high officials, everyone in their places. This was fine when the monarch was healthy. Formal royal beds were high off the ground and inconvenient for treating the sick. The king might suffer through a terminal illness on a much humbler, low trundle bed on wheels, but when death was imminent officials hastily moved him to the state bed, where he expired in a formal setting. Here, the newly deceased monarch would lie in state (the phrase originally meant lying in the state bed), carefully barbered and made up, as the public lined up to view the spectacle. When his successor assumed the throne he often began his coronation by descending from a bed set up in the adjoining arch-bishop's palace. Such was the power of monarchy in times when most people were illiterate and visual imagery was all-important, in life as well as death.

The royal bed was often protected by a balustrade, which ordinary people could not approach. A specially appointed guard was always present. There was an aura of divinity about the royal bed and the monarchy. Dogs were firmly kept away, except for royal pets, some of which were trained as foot warmers.

Trundle beds were common in royal bedrooms, for the monarch never slept alone. There was always a valet nearby. In the case of a queen, a maid of honor of good birth would occupy the trundle. Highborn courtiers were in attendance day and night. The humble trundle bed was often filled by a person of considerable rank. Other courtiers slept on *paillasses*, or straw mattresses, on the floor. The trundle beds rolled on casters (or trundles) so they could be pushed out of the way or even under the royal bed by day. The actual royal bed was often of such size that the king could invite a prominent man to share it for a night, perhaps as a gesture of favor, in an entirely platonic act.

Elaborately decorated beds also figured prominently and publicly in royal weddings. The bedding of the bride and groom and consummation of the marriage were surrounded with ceremony and often drunken revelry, numerous witnesses attending the bedding to verify the consummation of the marriage. If the newlywed couple did not go to bed and have sexual intercourse, the union could be annulled immediately. The bed itself could be elaborately decorated for the occasion and was sometimes a large platform. The marital bed constructed in 1430 for Philip the Good of Burgundy and Isabella of Portugal holds the Guinness world record for the largest functional bed: 5.79 meters long and 3.8 meters wide.[3]

MAJESTIC BEDS

Queen Elizabeth I's bed lay at the heart of her court. It was here that she rested and slept, away from the pressures of the day.[4] She had a stable of beds, all carefully furnished with luxurious fabrics and adorned with bright colors. When she embarked on a royal progress from palace to palace or noble house to noble house, her best bed often traveled with her. The carved wooden frame was elaborately painted and gilded. Silver and velvet adorned the valance, and exotic ostrich feathers topped the crimson satin headboard. Elizabeth slept behind tapestry curtains trimmed with gold and valuable buttons. Her beds were as much symbols of her power as places to sleep. Each one was elaborate and magnificent. At Whitehall she rested on a bed fabricated from a blend of colored woods, behind curtains of Indian-painted silk. When she visited Richmond Palace, she lay on a boat-shaped bed with curtains of "sea water green." Wherever the monarch rested, her bed was the bed of state. And wherever she went she required what were often called privy lodgings, where she was secluded from the court. These were a series of rooms—a Presence Chamber, a Privy Chamber, and a Bedchamber—which led off the main hall. Admittance to each chamber was a carefully measured statement of a person's access to the queen, a barometer of intimacy.

Elizabeth's court was an enormous institution, having more than a thousand servants and attendants. Brewers and bakers, cooks, tailors, and stable hands served a small army of courtiers and ambassadors. It was an itinerant organization, one which moved in vast processions between the four royal palaces at Whitehall, Hampton Court, Richmond, and Windsor. Three hundred carts were needed to move the furniture, tapestries, gowns, and ornaments from palace to palace. The court also traveled with the queen on visits away from the capital.

Reaching the Queen's Bedchamber, far from the hurly-burly of the court, required crossing well-defined and strictly controlled frontiers. The Presence Chamber was a large reception room with a throne and canopy of state. Ambassadors, courtiers, bishops, and suitors congregated there, hoping for a glimpse of the monarch. Elizabeth's Privy Chamber was where she spent most of her time, heavily guarded by a force of 146 Yeomen of the Guard. Here, she transacted government business, entertained guests, gossiped, and listened to music, occasionally with dancing. The Privy Chamber and Bedchamber led off the Presence Chamber. This was the center of the court and the most private place in the realm. Both the Privy and Bed chambers were the realm not of men but of women.

Only twenty-eight women served in the queen's private chambers during her entire reign. They were intimate friends of Her Majesty, some of whom had attended her at her coronation. The Ladies of the Privy and Bedchambers washed the queen, applied her makeup, and did her hair. They chose her clothes and jewelry and assisted her dressing. They also supervised the serving of her food and drink, checking it for poison and other harmful substances. Chamberers cleaned her rooms, emptied washbowls, and arranged her bed linen. Unmarried, highborn maids of honor dressed in white provided companionship and entertainment, especially dancing. All the women were expected to be in constant attendance, for the queen's needs were the highest priority. Even when ill or pregnant, they attended her, right up to the last few weeks before giving birth. Then they left their newborns to wet nurses and returned to duty almost immediately.

Elizabeth lived in a cocoon of favored women. They slept alongside her in bed or in a nearby truckle bed set in the dark chamber. The ladies were close bodyguards in a court riddled with factionalism, where the threat of assassination was always in the background. Closer to Her Majesty than anyone else, they knew her thoughts and changing moods, so much so that ambassadors and high officials sought their favor. A wise clerk of the Privy Council advised the queen's principal secretary, "Learn before you access Her Majesty's disposition by some in the Privy Chamber, with whom you must keep credit."[5]

The queen lived under intense, unrelenting scrutiny. In an age of short life expectancy and sudden death, ambassadors from other nations regularly sent home reports about her daily behavior and state of heath. She had suffered from ill health since puberty, including chronic indigestion and insomnia, and there was widespread concern about her potential marriage partners and her fertility. Women were thought at the time to have much stronger sexual appetites than men, which made it hard to believe that any of them, especially an unmarried woman, would willingly remain chaste. Diplomatic rumors revolved around her potential infertility at a time when the security of the still-fragile Protestant realm depended on her marrying and bearing an heir. The frequency of her periods was a matter for international reporting and speculation.

Each morning, wherever the queen was residing or visiting, her ladies drew back the bed curtains. She would usually remain in bed as the routine of cleaning and lighting fires took place. Then she would have breakfast in her night things before taking a fast walk in the garden or reading by the window. Washing, makeup, and dressing could take hours. As she engaged in informal conversation with them, the ladies pinned her into her elaborate, heavy gowns. Next, they added the jewelry, which lay in coffers covered in velvet and embroidered with gold. The royal valuables were as secure as they could be in her Bedchamber. Finally, an iron shoehorn eased shoes onto her feet. Only then was the queen ready to enter the Presence and Privy Chambers, where she would be on public display.

The monarch's existence was choreographed to the centimeter. Even meals were accompanied by elaborate ceremony, for it was considered unseemly for her to eat in public except at banquets. At the end of the day she would retire to the Bedchamber to wash and disrobe. Her ladies checked the mattresses and bedlinen for bugs and hidden daggers, and the room was searched for intruders. The queen would then climb into bed, where she reclined on layers of mattresses of straw, flock, and feathers, the softest being, of course, at the top. Silk sheets adorned with her royal arms and the Tudor rose covered Her Majesty. The window was closed to keep out dangerous night air, the bed curtains drawn, and the queen was locked into her Bedchamber.

Only once did a male enter the women's world of the chamber without official permission. The Earl of Essex, long a royal favorite, but filthy after a hasty journey from Ireland, entered the royal apartment at Nonsuch Palace in Surrey in 1599, where he crossed the bedroom threshold. He glimpsed Elizabeth wigless, half-dressed, and without her makeup. The speechless queen behaved graciously as he knelt and begged for forgiveness. A day later Essex was placed under house arrest. In 1601 he was executed for treason.

Security surrounded royal bedchambers even when the monarch was away, and for good reason. At Versailles a valet always sat inside the wooden enclosure around the king's bed because the court was concerned about sorcery. An enemy of the monarch could sprinkle spell-carrying mixtures on the bed that could endanger the occupant. In 1600 a woman named Nicole Mignon was burned alive for trying to arrange the poisoning of King Henry IV of France. Three years earlier an upholsterer "of the rue du Temple" was convicted of "the intention to murder the king." He was hanged and his body burned.

∎

Royal beds were prominent features of births, christenings, marriages, and deaths. The beds where royal mothers-to-be lay were often elaborately decorated with rich hangings, the cost of the bed receiving more public attention than the baby's weight. Like all pregnant mothers-to-be, they were expected to receive their friends while in bed, though things were taken to extremes. Balls were sometimes held in their presence. Royal births were highly public matters for the court, involving elaborate protocols for those in attendance. Witnesses had to include princes and princesses of the blood, secretaries of state and other high officials, all looking on to ensure that there was no fraud. These measures did not always prevent malicious gossip. Mary of Modena, the Catholic consort of King James II, gave birth to a son in 1688 in the presence of numerous ministers and courtiers. But rumors, motivated by powerful anti-Catholic sentiment and dread of a future Catholic monarch, soon spread that a live male infant had been smuggled into the bedroom in a warming pan to replace the queen's stillborn son. The stories ultimately contributed to the overthrow of James II, who was replaced in 1688 by the resolutely Protestant William II.

One major advantage of bedrooms is that even minute nuances of respect could be noticed. When Cardinal Richelieu met with the English ambassador in 1625 to negotiate the marriage of King Charles I and Henrietta of France, an absurd dispute arose over the number of steps across the floor to be taken by each of the meeting's participants. Richelieu solved the problem by conducting the gathering from his bed, which changed the protocol rules.

The king whom Richelieu served as chief minister, Louis XIII, was a chronic stutterer of sour character who was far more interested in hawking and hunting than in governing. The two men turned France into an absolute monarchy, but Louis had simple tastes, remarkable for a king of his background. For most of his reign he used only two beds, one painted black with silver ornamentation, the other purple and gold. Compare this with Gabrielle de'Estrées, the mistress of his father, Henry IV, who had twelve lavishly appointed beds just for use in winter. Jean-Baptiste Poquelin, the satirical playwright and actor known as Molière, was valet of the king's chamber under Louis, an inherited post his father had purchased. He didn't share the king's tastes but he did sleep in a lavish bed with bronze eagle feet, a carved and gilded headboard, and floral brocade curtains. He also owned eighteen elaborate nightgowns. There were few feminine touches around Louis XIII's bedroom, as his marriage to Anne of Spain was unhappy, and they were usually apart. Louis never took mistresses. In 1638, however, after four stillbirths, the couple finally had a son, the future Louis XIV, who ascended to the throne in 1641 at the age of three and reigned for seventy-two years.

ROYAL PROTOCOL

Louis XIV, known as the Sun King, firmly believed in the divine right of kings, which gave him a mandate to turn France into a centralized kingdom governed from the Palace of Versailles.[6] The nobles he drew to his court were forced to wait on him day and night if they wished to enjoy pensions and other privileges. As the center of all attention Louis XIV was under constant public observation. He entertained the nobility every day, lavishing them with ceremonies and other expensive distractions but kept them firmly under his scrutiny. His central control lessened the power of the aristocracy and reduced the chronic civil wars that had plagued his predecessors. Above all, he effectively ruled France and ran military campaigns from his bed. Beds were the stages on which he performed, and he was obsessed with them.

The bed inventories of Louis XIV describe at least twenty-five different designs. The royal bed storeroom at Versailles held at least four hundred beds, many named after the tapestries that adorned them. One, called Le Triomphe de Venus, consumed the talents of the tapestry master Simon Delobel for twelve years. The king regularly gave beds as presents to his offspring, even one to his physician. He is said to have enjoyed a flirtation with mirrors set on the undersides of his bed canopies, instead of the usual erotic paintings, to encourage his more restrained guests. When an energetic lover in one such bed caused a mirror to shatter and nearly kill him, the royal experiment ended abruptly.

Inevitably, bed decoration and gilding became ever more elaborate, following Louis's lead and the winds of fashion. The king eventually forbade registrars, notaries, attorneys, merchants, and artisans and their wives from owning any form of gilded furniture, including beds adorned with gold or silver. The penalties included fines and confiscation of the offending items, but no one seems to have observed the rule for long.

Like many royals before him, Louis XIV lived in public. His life recalled that of an Egyptian pharaoh, every minute aspect of whose daily routine was regimented and organized. The Greek historian Diodorus Siculus wrote of a pharaoh in the first century BC that there was a set time for sleeping with his wife.[7] So it was with Louis, who held court in his bedchamber at Versailles throughout his long reign, and whose ritual risings and retirings, the *levée* and *couchée*, were integral to his rule. "With an almanac and a watch, you could be three hundred leagues from here and say what he [the king] was doing," wrote Louis's godchild, the gossipy Duke of Saint-Simon.[8] The king's day followed a routine as strict as that of court, which allowed his officials to plan their days accordingly. From his bed Louis made decisions, issued decrees, and received anyone lucky enough to gain this privileged access to his semidivine self, a group that included not only courtiers and extended family but also his illegitimate descendants, to Saint-Simon's horrified disapproval.

The Sun King's rising and setting were as predictable as the movements of the sun itself, and he even remodeled his bedchamber to face its first glow. His official awakening, at the hands of the

King Louis XIV's bed at Versailles.

first valet of the Chamber, came at about 8:30 a.m., even if he had been up for some time. The first doctor and the first surgeon attended him, and then a private gathering followed, open to a select few that included his childhood nurse, who always gave him a kiss. The king was washed, combed, and shaved (every other day) in front of this audience. The officers of the Chamber and of the Clothes Storehouse attended the king while he was dressed and drank soup for breakfast. The grand getting-up ceremony saw the bed curtains drawn back, witnessed by the grand chamberlain, close royal servants, and important members of the court, who had paid for the privilege of being there. They watched from behind the gilded balustrade separating the bed from the rest of the bedchamber. This was the moment when a noble could have a quick, deferential word with the monarch, a symbolic moment of accessibility and intimacy.

As the morning wore on, the bedchamber grew more crowded. By the time the king was putting on his shoes and stockings the onlookers included his arts event organizers and his ministers and secretaries. At the fifth entrée, women were admitted for the first time, and at the sixth, the king's legitimate and illegitimate children and their spouses. As many as a hundred people might crowd into the room.

Meanwhile, a procession had formed in the Hall of Mirrors next to the royal apartments. At 10:00 a.m. Louis crossed the state apartments followed by his courtiers. The crowd often pressed around him, slipping him pieces of paper or seeking a brief word. Half an hour later he attended Mass in the Royal Chapel. By 11:00 he was back in his apartment conducting government business brought by five or six of his ministers. By 1:00 the monarch was eating alone in his bedchamber at a table facing the window. Theoretically this was a solitary meal, but he invariably invited members of the court to watch him eat. At 2:00 the king announced his plans for the next day before going for a walk or carriage ride or indulging in his favorite sport, hunting in the park or riding on horseback in the surrounding forest. He was back by 6:00. The early evening was devoted to an evening gathering and entertainment as well as official papers. By 10:00 he was back in his bedchamber's antechamber, where a crowd would squeeze in to watch him eat his grand public supper, surrounded by members of the royal family. The king then retired to his private quarters to talk more freely with close friends and family. At 11:30 the going-to-bed ceremony, the couchée, began, the reverse of the morning ritual. The Sun King symbolically set at the end of the day. He died in his bedchamber after a reign of seventy-two years. The Palace of Versailles was a statement of absolute rule, of the power of Louis XIV as the distant, infallible, central force of the realm. Even the formal gardens, flawlessly designed and maintained, spoke of his commanding power. The royal bedchamber lay on the palace's upper floor, centrally located along the huge building's east-facing wall. This was the most important room in the palace, the place where the Sun King rose and set and from which his decisions and decrees spread their light over all of France.

BED BOARDROOMS

The Sun King's successor, Louis XV, had but one bed and banished most of his great-grandfather's bedroom ceremony. The English art historian and politician Harold Walpole, who was presented at the fifteenth Louis's court in 1765, reported that he was ushered into the royal bedroom as the king was putting on his shirt. Apparently, the monarch "[talks] good humouredly to a few, glares at strangers, goes to mass, to dinner, and a-hunting." The queen was in the same room, at a dressing table attended by "two or three old ladies."[9]

Louis XV's ceremonial bedchamber was a majestic but impractical setting for a man who cherished his privacy. He built a new chamber in 1738 that was smaller and easier to heat, as it faced south. The bed stood in an alcove, a feature of elaborate bedchambers said to have originated in Spain. Separated from the room by a balustrade, often with columns, an alcove was really a room within the chamber. Louis's alcove contained seats as well, so that he could use it for small receptions. A century later they were smaller, secluded, and had more discreet uses.

The king's most beloved mistress was the Marquise de Pompadour, who lived in a four-room apartment in the central part of the palace from 1745 to 1751. Louis could enter her bedchamber from his private apartment. A later mistress, Countess du Barry, occupied another lavish apartment whose bedchamber was accessible via a hidden staircase.

Royal bedchambers were by now formal places, where the bed was rarely slept in and where enthusiastic sex happened rarely, if ever. One can more accurately describe them as a kind of formal boardroom, a place where royal decisions were made. What mattered was access. To see the monarch in his undergarments or conversing in bed was a high honor, granted only to the most ambitious and prominent courtiers and officers of state. The bed itself was a symbol of the splendor of the monarchy that served to impress visitors. Some were symbols of true magnificence, like the bed Queen Anne commissioned as she was dying in 1714. It was almost 5½ meters high, built of 57 parts, and adorned with yellow and crimson velvet hangings and extremely expensive silk mattresses. It cost the enormous sum of £674, at the time as much as a moderate-sized London townhouse. No one has ever slept on it. Even the more practical traveling bed made for the Prince of Wales in 1716, before he became George II, was an elaborate production. It breaks down into 54 pieces, complete with mattresses and hangings. As late as 1771 elaborate royal beds were commonplace. Few, however, rivaled the state bed of Queen Charlotte, consort of King George III, which was embroidered exquisitely by the ladies of Phoebe White's School for Orphaned Women, a charity supported by the queen.

With Queen Victoria's accession to the British throne in 1837 the royal bedroom door was firmly closed. Victoria's intense privacy was a reflection of a more inhibited age in which bedrooms and beds were hidden away from public view. Only a few rules lingered, among them the presence of the foreign secretary at royal births, a custom that finally ended with the birth of the present Prince Charles in 1948.

Elaborately decorated beds remained fashionable, especially among the wealthy and among Eastern potentates. Perhaps it was because we spend so much of our lives in them, and, after all, why not repose among the luxurious trappings of wealth and fine art? Few beds rival that of Saddiq Muhammed Khan Abassi IV, the nawab of Bahawalpur in what is now Pakistan. In 1882 he ordered a silver-encrusted bed from Maison Christofle in Paris, a company that was (and remains) legendary for silver gilding and fine tableware and was accustomed to dealing with royalty like the sultan of Turkey as well as noble families throughout Europe and Asia. Maison Christofle decorated the Elysée Palace and provided the tableware and furnishings for the Orient Express from 1860 to 1940. For Abassi they built a bed of "dark wood decorated with applied sterling with gilded parts, monograms . . . ornamented with four life-size bronze figures of naked females painted in flesh colours with natural hair, movable eyes and arms holding fans and horse tails."[10] These decorations required 290 kilograms of silver. The four figures, depicting women from France, Greece, Italy, and Spain, were each given appropriate hair colors and skin tones. Clever mechanisms allowed the nawab to set the figures to winking while they fanned him. A music box built into the bed played thirty seconds of Gounod's *Faust*. After his death the bed vanished. It was eventually traced to the Abassi family's Sadiq Garh Palace at Bahawalpur. When the last nawab died in 1966 the prime minister ordered an inventory of all his possessions. The bed lay in the palace's Silver Bedroom for years, while the palace and its contents were sealed during a legal dispute between the nawab's heirs. In 1992 the bed went missing.

Abassi never ruled from his royal bed but kept it purely private. The public bedchamber and ruling from bed were very much a European phenomenon. No monarch now rules his or her domain from a bed of state. The royal crib lies outside the public eye. Only rarely do beds now figure prominently in history, and then only as backdrops, not as statements of divinely sanctioned authority. Throughout the Second World War Winston Churchill governed Great Britain from his bed with a mixture of eccentricity and panache, which sometimes led to confusion and downright disorder. Britain's top military man, Field Marshall Lord Alanbrooke, spent many hours in Churchill's bedrooms and complained in his diary of the challenges of dealing with the prime minister. A common encounter came on January 27, 1942: "This interview was typical of many future ones of this kind. The scene in his bedroom was always the same and I only wish some artist could have committed it to canvas. The red and gold dressing gown in itself was worth going miles to see, and only Winston would have thought of wearing it! He looked rather like some Chinese Mandarin! The few hairs were usually ruffled on his bald head. A large cigar stuck sideways out of his face. The bed was littered with papers and dispatches. Sometimes the tray with his finished breakfast was still on the bed table. The bell was continually being rung for secretaries, typists, stenographers, or his faithful valet Sawyers."

History does not relate whether Churchill conducted meetings from his bed as a way of keeping important officials off balance. He was certainly capable of it, but a greater contrast with Louis XIV's choreographed levée and couchée is hard to imagine.[11]

NINE

A Private Refuge

And so, having given witness to the whole evolution of the bed, we come to your own. If you are like most westerners, your bed will be hidden away in your bedroom, typically on an upper floor or toward the back of your house. Steeped in notions of privacy, sexuality, and sleep, your bedroom is likely a place where only a select few have set foot and seen your bed. When the young British artist Tracey Emin presented her messy bed (see the frontispiece) to the public in the late 1990s it caused outrage. The critic Jonathan Jones tartly wondered in 2008 if there was anything more to the artist than her willingness to reveal private trauma. Yet in 1616, when Shakespeare bequeathed his wife of thirty-four years his "second best bed," it was no snub but rather a tender gesture as the marital bed they shared. In his day the best bed was commonly kept in the main living space so that visitors could admire it—and appreciate your wealth at having two beds. How is it that our beds have gone private?

SEEKING PRIVACY

When the internet pioneer Vint Cerf of Google suggested in 2013 that privacy is a modern anomaly, savage criticism descended upon him.[1] Historically, however, he was perfectly correct. What we call privacy, with its ideas of individual secrecy and seclusion from the public realm, is only about 150 years old, although it has much older roots. Interestingly, the appearance of the modern bedroom also dates back only about two centuries. Until the Industrial Revolution, privacy was not a priority in any human society. In relation to money, prestige, security, and convenience, solitude took a distant backseat.

In prehistoric times the need for warmth and protection prevented much privacy. People lay close to the hearth or huddled together. In all likelihood children saw their parents having sex, for they slept close by or in the same small hut. Bronislaw Malinowski's classic report on Trobriand Islanders' sex lives in 1929 observed that adults took no special precautions to prevent their children from seeing them having sex.[2] They merely rebuked them if they stared and told them to cover their heads with a mat. On the other hand, sex in traditional hunter-gatherer and subsistence farming societies often took place outside the sleeping spaces, where there wasn't an audience and was perhaps more freedom of movement. Nevertheless, for people who lived in inhospitable environments or landscapes where carnivores abounded, the absence of privacy was a cheap price to pay for survival. Among traditional Arctic societies, to seek solitude outside was considered very dangerous, indeed stupid.

No one knows when privacy first became a concept. Perhaps it arose with the widening gap between rulers, nobility, and everyone else. Ancient Egyptian pharaohs slept on elevated beds, as did prominent officials; everyone else lay on mats or the ground. Ancient Athenians were good at architectural geometry and sometimes designed houses to offer maximum exposure to light while minimizing exposure to public view. Even the Roman word *privatus*, from whence our word *private*, was typically used simply to mean a citizen without public office and derives from the word *privo*, or "I bereave, deprive" but also "I free, release."

Then, as today, privacy seems to have been controversial. Some savants, like Socrates, disapproved of people hiding themselves away in the interest of gaining privacy. He is reported to have remarked of such solitude, "No man will ever rightly gain either his due honor or office," even justice. The far less egalitarian Romans enjoyed displaying their wealth, be it lavish rural villas, elaborate fishponds, or urban mansions. Rich people's residences were often virtually museums for the curious. Pliny the Elder, in AD 77, wrote of the great fortune of the rich that "allows nothing to be concealed . . . their bedrooms and intimate retreats . . . and exposes to talk all the arcane secrets."[3] In fact, many larger Roman houses did not have specified bedrooms, but instead portable beds that could be moved from one vacant chamber to another.

The Romans hid nothing in their public baths, and the attached latrines were communal places where people sat side by side, the archaeology offering only occasional hints of any cubicle-type divisions. To relieve themselves they sat on U-shaped holes in benches, then wiped with rags or shared sponges on sticks, all the while engaging in unembarrassed conversation. The latrines were sociable, communal meeting places. For all the luxury and display enjoyed by the privileged, most Roman city-dwellers lived in crowded, often jerry-built apartments where privacy was nonexistent. Few people cared. Sex with "public" prostitutes was (for men) not a fumbling secret but an open source of pleasure. Witness a graffito at Pompeii: "Baths, drink, and sex corrupt our bodies, but baths, drink, and sex make life worth living."[4] Privacy was not a priority elsewhere in the world either. The Chinese *kangs*, the mat-covered heated masonry platforms that appear as early as 5000 BC, were never private bedrooms but places where several people slept, ate, and socialized. By 1000 BC sleeping on the floor gradually gave way to raised beds. The elaborately carved and gilded bedchambers of the elite, more furniture displays than retreats, became places where one both slept and entertained guests. Some had places for storing clothes.

There was one facet of human life, however, where secrecy and seclusion perhaps always abounded: religion. As archaeologists, we see privacy in almost every religious setup—from the layout of Iron Age Yemeni temples with their tripartite sanctuaries always hidden at the back, to the secret mummification rites of Egyptian priests, to the great Ice Age cave art buried deep in inaccessible cave systems. With secrecy come power and the illusion of divine agency. Christianity was one of the most powerful catalysts for the Western version of privacy. Seclusion, following Christ's epochal forty days in the wilderness, was a central tenet of Christian ideas. With their obsessions with mortality and sin in a world where evil was everywhere, the extremely devout withdrew from society, even from monastic communities, and contemplated God and human existence away from the distractions of the world. The fourth-century Christian monk St. Anthony of Egypt remarked that "like a fish going towards the sea, we must hurry to reach our cell, for fear that if we delay outside, we will lose our interior watchfulness." Fasting and asceticism became fashionable, the most extreme practitioners being Egyptian hermits who lived in remote desert caves. Another ascetic writer, St. Anthony's contemporary John Cassian, described his austere diet of dry biscuits, drops of oil, and occasional vegetables or small fish. One modern researcher estimates that this diet provided about 930 calories a day. "The more the body becomes emaciated," Cassian wrote, "the more the soul grows." If they strictly followed their starvation diet, they would have reached complete chastity in about six months. Their solitude was not a quest for privacy but a form of atonement for Christ's suffering on the cross. There was, as we've said, no Latin nor indeed medieval word for privacy. There was, however, *privation*, "taking away."[5] Moreover, while Queen Elizabeth I may have been keen on her privy, the word derives from the Old French *privé*, or a friendly and intimate place. Rather, privacy assumed a more modern dimension in the Renaissance, beginning with a pronouncement of the Fourth Council of Lateran, the Great Council of 1215, that made confession compulsory for everyone. Under this rubric, consciousness of one's sins was a form of internal morality, acquired by contemplation and exposed only in the privacy of confession. Reading was encouraged, especially after the printing press revolutionized access to learning. What each person read fostered greater individualism throughout Europe. Religious groups like the Dutch Brethren of the Common Life published widely read religious texts promoting a simple devotion to Christ. Their teachings urged artists, poets, and theologians to abandon worldly things and turn their hearts toward God. Carthusian monks had individual cells and lived under a rule of silence to encourage contemplation. Individual moral governance gradually turned inward, became private, more solitary.

BUILDING DIVISIONS

As late as the sixteenth century, dwellings with one large room heated by a fire pit and central brick chimney were commonplace, preferred because they were the best way of keeping people warm in winter. One such house, in Newport, Rhode Island, was built in 1732. It belonged to the uncle of our editor, Bill Frucht, who recalled that it had seven rooms on two floors, each with its own fireplace that fed into a central chimney that formed the core of the house. The wealthy might live in private houses or have separate chambers, but it was more convenient and warmer to keep the entire household, including servants, in close quarters. Privacy was still minimal. Witness the testimony of a servant of the Italian marquis

Albergati Capacelli, who served his master for eleven years. In a case brought by his master's wife requesting annulment of her marriage on the grounds of incontinence, he testified in 1751 that "on three or four occasions I saw the said marquis getting out of bed with a perfect erection of the male organ."[6]

Beds, in Capacelli's era, were places where one could indeed rest and read but almost certainly with company. Beds were a logical gathering place and also a place where guests might well spend the night with most or all of the family. They were, like royal beds, effectively public places. Single beds first became popular in hospitals, where patients had long shared beds, especially children, who were crammed close to one another regardless of their medical condition. Contagious diseases spread like wildfire under these conditions.

Domesticity and privacy first came to prominence during the late eighteenth century. Male hangouts had by then moved outside the home to clubs and coffeehouses, gin shops and street gatherings, while (respectable) women stayed in the background. A combination of powerful forces turned the home into a place of refuge and renewal in a changing, increasingly stressful world. The rise of Evangelical Christianity, with its belief in the power of the family to maintain good relationships both within its own circle and without, was an important factor. Christian homes became microcosms of love and generosity in reaction to the increasingly harsh and ruthless world of the workplace. Men came home to a harmonious environment that surrounded them with love and serenity. Christian origins apart, the idea became so ingrained that it became a secular norm.

The Industrial Revolution turned most Europeans into city dwellers. In 1800 only 20 percent of Great Britain's population lived in cities. A century later that percentage had climbed to nearly 80 percent, and London was the largest city in the world, with over four million inhabitants. Most of the city's small, terraced dwellings that are still ubiquitous today were built in the decades surrounding 1900. These houses were a search for separation and retirement from others within an increasingly hectic city. In Paris the story was the same. Despite its promiscuous growth, in 1900 perhaps as many as two-thirds of all French workers worked at home. Today, nearly all Europeans work outside the house.

The workplace had changed fundamentally: factories, fixed hours, and much more regimented work environments had become the rule.[7] The move out of the home affected laborers and professionals alike. Doctors who had maintained consulting rooms in their residences now had separate offices. Women, who might previously have helped their shopkeeping husbands at the counter or by doing the accounts, now lived separate lives centered on the home. They became homemakers.

As the nineteenth century unfolded, many people moved out to the suburbs while continuing to work in the city center. This separation became a philosophy, to the point where working men often were two people—the one at work, the other at home: two lives, two completely different individuals. A popular self-help pamphlet written in 1908 by Arnold Bennett, optimistically entitled "How to live on twenty-four hours a day," makes just this distinction. Bennett suggests that the average man has no autonomy over his working day, and only outside that time can he really live. His main recommendation is to read ancient philosophy rather than waste time on the newspaper. The father of the art critic and writer John Ruskin drew a contrast between the dreariness of society and "the circle of my own Fire Side with my Love sitting opposite irradiating all around her, and my most extraordinary boy."[8] This separation of the elements of one's life extended into home. No longer were there multipurpose rooms where furniture was moved around. (The French word for furniture—*meuble*—means "movable.") Now each room was segregated for different activities, both socially and in terms of the hierarchy between employer and servant. For the first time bedrooms became commonplace.

DISCRETE BEDROOMS

By the nineteenth century sleeping in specific bedrooms had become commonplace in wealthy Western homes. No longer did servants routinely sleep with the family or bed down en masse in halls or kitchens. Each had separate bed quarters. Throughout the entire home realm a woman was, in Victorian terms, a "ministering angel to domestic bliss." She ruled the household, although her authority was derived from her husband. Nowhere was this belief better projected than in the middle-class bedroom. Whereas these rooms had once served as sitting rooms as well as sleeping places, they were now sleeping places alone. Victorians believed that the more specialist rooms a house had, the better, which meant that the wife and husband might have separate, perhaps interconnected bedrooms, each with an adjoining dressing room. The mistress of such a house might seek refuge in her private boudoir, from the French *bouder*, "to sulk."

Architect magazine published an authoritative essay in 1875 declaring that bedrooms were only for sleeping. Any other use was unwholesome, immoral, and contrary to the principle that every important aspect of life required a separate room. Yet it was not just that communal sleeping was immoral—requiring even the smallest urban house to have two bedrooms, one for the parents and one for the children—there were also health concerns. With the rise in urban populations the nineteenth century was fraught with anxieties about public health. Many still believed that diseases were generated spontaneously from foul water or air, making the sleeping, stagnant body particularly worrisome. The doctor B. W. Richardson recommended in 1880 that adults not share a bed with their children lest they suck the "vital warmth" from the offspring.

Separate rooms added to the merchandising opportunities in an increasingly commercialized world. The mass marketing of childhood—including children's toys and furniture—began with the Victorians. Targeting children has shallow roots: even the supposedly age-old convention of blue for boys' toys, clothes, furniture and pink for girls (requiring parents to buy double the stuff), was codified only after the Second World War. As a fashion-trade article from 1918 explained, "The generally accepted rule is pink for the boys, and blue for the girls. The reason is that pink, being a more decided and stronger color, is more suitable for the boy, while blue, which is more delicate and dainty, is prettier for the girl."[9]

The separation of functions had not yet touched the lives of the urban poor. Crowded into squalid rooms and crowded apartment buildings, they still lived in public. If a woman fell sick, the entire street knew about it, as she often lay in bed in full view of the household. Debates over privacy intensified. In December 1890 the *Harvard Law Review* published an article by Louis Brandeis, soon to become a Supreme Court Justice, on the right to privacy, arguing that because of the intensity and complexity "attendant on advancing civilization . . . solitude and privacy have become more essential to the individual."[10] The court had ruled in 1868 that privacy was a way for a man to maintain ownership over his wife's public and private life—including his right to abuse her physically.

In a century when the British Empire encompassed much of the world, Victorian values and housekeeping practices became deeply engrained in remote lands, from Australia and New Zealand through Asia and much of tropical Africa. Colonial administrators took their furniture and house-decorating ideas with them, along with their bedrooms, beds, and bedding. By the late nineteenth century middle-class ideas of privacy, especially privacy in the bedroom, were also deeply engrained in the United States. Two centuries earlier New England houses had a ground floor hall where cooking, eating, and a variety of other household activities took place. Then there was the parlor, where the family kept their most prized possessions: the "best bed" along with the finest table and chairs. This was where the husband and wife slept, as the most important people in the house. Space within the family home was divided according to the meaning and value of what it encompassed, not on the basis of different activities.

By the eighteenth century passages and stairways had come into fashion, making movement through the house much easier. People routinely slept in actual bedrooms, complete with bed curtains, chairs, and curtains with matching fabrics. These were rooms for sleeping, resting quietly, and socializing with close relatives and friends. Births and deaths found people gathering in bedrooms for formal receptions.

SEPARATE BEDS

By the nineteenth century beds and mattresses had come a long way from the hay- or straw-stuffed sacks of medieval times. Sleeping alone was still almost unheard of. As we have seen, bed sharing persisted into the nineteenth century despite the Victorian household's obsession with privacy. A major catalyst of separation came with the development of internal staircases and hallways, which allowed servants and others to go to different rooms without passing through others.[11] Once, servants had slept in their master's or mistresses' bedrooms. Now they had their own quarters upstairs or downstairs and were summoned by bells. State power no longer resided in the royal bedroom but in legislatures and government offices, which meant that the bedrooms became less opulent and much more private.

In these private, distinct bedrooms couples often began to have their distinct beds. Two beds were a good way to avoid "fusty" infection and also underscored the Victorian ideas of modesty. These notions persisted long into the twentieth century. When Hollywood created its censorship guide in the 1930s, called the Hays Code, it decreed that on-screen couples must sleep in separate beds and, if kissing, one partner must keep a foot on the floor at all times. In the 1960s Sears and other large department stores continued to advertise twin beds for married couples, and it was not until the 1970s that such beds were seen as old-fashioned and prudish.

Recent research suggests that couples often sleep better when they sleep apart.[12] This is particularly true for those who sleep with noisy or restless partners, as noted by Courtine's unhappy wife, Sylvia, in Thomas Otway's play *The Atheist* (1684), in which she defines the typical husband as "heavy and useless, comes faint and loth to bed, turns about, grunts, snores." Such complaints explain why an estimated 30 or 40 percent of today's couples sleep apart, possibly including Donald and Melania Trump. "They have separate bedrooms," an anonymous source told *Us Weekly*. "They never spend the night together—ever." This was countered by another supposed insider source who asserted that they sleep in the same room but in separate beds, adding, "It's very 'royal' of them!"

ADVICE ON THE BEDROOM

The demand for multiple specialist rooms caused architects to puzzle over the relationship between bedrooms and other parts of the house. Nineteenth-century bedrooms, especially those of the husband and wife, were often on the ground floor and linked to the more public reception rooms. The notion was to separate family from servants, adults from children, older offspring from babies. Other members of the household slept on the second floor, and servants on higher floors. Status declined with the number of stairs one had to climb. This continued for generations, but eventually the entire ground floor was given over to daily living, with all sleeping rooms upstairs, each opening onto a corridor if there was space. Privacy was enhanced. But what could one do with the bedrooms in a single-story house or a city apartment? Two options came into popular use. One grouped bedrooms in a block along a corridor. The other had the bedrooms opening into the more social spaces. In small houses one bedroom served the parents, the other the children. Servants slept in the kitchen, which was often in the basement.

A steady stream of self-help books advised the young Victorian housewife about her bedrooms. Writing in 1888, the redoubtable and opinionated Jane Ellen Panton, the daughter of a well-known artist, urged housewives to escape the "orthodox bedrooms" of their youth, like hers of the 1850s and 1860s: "fearful" wallpaper, "all blue roses and yellow lilies, or what was worse still, the dreary drab and orange, or green upon green scrolls and foliage."[13] Victorian bedroom furniture was often shabby, having been recycled from the main rooms. Once a piece showed signs of further wear, it would move again, to the nursery or the servants' quarters.

Such transposing was particularly true of rugs, which progressed through many rooms as they became increasingly threadbare. Bedroom rugs were often castoffs from long and faithful service in the living room. They finally ended up as strips in the servants' bedrooms. No one expected visitors to inspect the master bedroom, so it didn't matter what it looked like. "I'm afraid I'm not an orthodox housekeeper," Panton declared. She advised her fictional housewife, the newly married Angelina, to buy "colours that give her pleasure." People are affected by their surroundings, she reasoned, and one was sometimes ill in one's bedroom. The paint used on doors and mantelpiece should match the wall colorings.[14]

Most houses had private bedrooms for the husband and wife as well as separate bedrooms for the children. Wealthy couples would not dream of sharing a bed and would have separate bedrooms. Window shades and blinds came into fashion. These were needed at a time when bedrooms still saw many tasks performed that are today undertaken in the bathroom. A washstand and mirror were de rigueur, a couch or chaise longue desirable. Washstands came with towel rails and sometimes with tiled backs to catch splashing water as you washed in the washbasin, which had been carefully filled by a maid or manservant. Servants laboriously carried hot water from the kitchen in brass or copper toilet cans for basins and portable hip baths. There was usually a central table, a table for toiletries, some chairs, also a small bookcase. Chamber pots were commonplace before the widespread use of the flush toilet. Commodes, that is, chairs or boxes containing a chamber pot, were commonplace in bedrooms until the early 1900s, which brought interior lavatories. Panton recommended wardrobes, if you could find them, and a "long chair," a type of camp bed that could be used as a couch or armchair, for when life became overwhelming. Screens were considered essential, both to hide the bed and to combat drafts.

Lighting was always a problem. Many advisers counseled against gaslights in bedrooms, for they depleted the oxygen in the room. A single candle brought up when retiring was strongly recommended. Affluent households would have a double stick on the mantelpiece and one on the dressing table. A box of safety matches in an accessible place was essential, as finding them in the dark could be a problem. As always, Mrs. Panton had the solution: nail a box over the bed, paint it, and put a picture above.

There was also the problem of where to keep one's clothes. For a start, clothes hangers as we know them were not in general use until the twentieth century, when they became known as "shoulders." People simply hung their clothes on hooks in wardrobes or used trunks or boxes. Almost all bedroom furniture had storage space for clothes. The bulky dresses worn by Victorian women presented a serious challenge. "For ball-dresses . . . and ordinary dresses," Panton advised using box ottomans covered with attractive fabrics and numerous small cupboards, which could be placed anywhere and were useful for storing boots and shoes, so they did not lie loose on the floor.[15]

Crowds of well-meaning advisers stood ready to define what constituted a bedroom. Everyone sleeps, of course, but many advisers stressed individuality. One expert, Ella Church, remarked in 1877 that one could tell a mother's room at a glance: it had an extra large, comfortable bed, an easy chair, and a table. Everything was set up for "accommodating numerous inmates." Bachelors' rooms would be crammed with newspapers, pipes, cigars, and photographs of actresses. Grandmother's bedroom would have an old-fashioned four-poster bedspread, a tall bureau, and a favorite comfortable chair. The bedroom was where one expressed one's individuality and kept one's personal possessions, "those numberless little things which are such sure indications of individual character." The master bedroom was an exception, for, though it was shared with the husband, it tended to stress the wife's needs, with such furnishings as a dressing table and a long mirror.

Individuality was one thing, health another. Many mid-nineteenth-century American interior design writers discouraged bed curtains, wallpapers, and carpets because they gathered dust and made rooms hard to clean. More people began to advocate fresh air and good air circulation. A bedroom facing south was thought to attract the healthiest breezes. Some authors recommended that people sleep facing east so that the body was lined up on the sun's path. The *Ladies' Home Journal* and other publications encouraged sleeping on screened porches located just outside the bedroom. One could sleep in a specially designed sleeping bag or in a special fresh-air tent that fitted around the window and extended over the sleeper's head. A window on the bedroom side allowed the occupant to converse with people in the bedroom. Husband, wife, and children might all share the same sleeping porch.

An 1886 advertisement for Maple of London's bedroom furniture, including a white bedroom suite and "iron and brass four-post bedsteads."

Bedroom furniture became more commonplace during the mid-nineteenth century. The décor became more carefully designed and always centered around the bed, which could be simple or an elaborate four-poster. Lighting, always a problem, relied mainly on candles, which were extremely dangerous in bed, especially if a reader fell asleep. Panton suggested a candle lantern and strategically placed gas brackets on the walls to provide maximum light. She also liked a few indoor plants in her décor and advised sleeping with at least a little window open at night. The whole bedroom should be "pretty, tasteful, and quiet," as carefully furnished and thought out as the dining and living rooms. Everything should be "very nice."

CARE OF THE BED

The bed was arguably the most labor-intensive item of furniture in the nineteenth-century home. By the 1860s four-posters were going out of fashion. Brass or iron beds were strongly recommended by many authorities, as they were easier to keep bug-free. As wood and metal bed platforms came into use, they were overlain by layers of blankets, quilts, sheets, and multiple feather, horsehair, and straw mattresses. Panton hated wooden bedsteads, citing "immense trouble with certain small animals that came there mysteriously," requiring the beds to be taken apart, scrubbed, and reassembled.[16] And if someone with an infectious disease slept in the bed the answer was "a bonfire." Panton favored brass or iron bedsteads, which were "clean and healthy." She herself slept on a spring mattress made entirely of finely woven chains, which worked much better than "old-fashioned spring beds," whose spiral springs squeaked whenever one turned over: "One is restless and cannot sleep." One Victorian householder's manual prescribed an iron bedstead, a thick brown sheet to cover the metal springs, three or four blankets, an eiderdown, and pillow covers. The author recommended turning the mattress every morning and changing the pillowcase twice a day, ornate ones being used at night, plain ones during the day.

The ultimate authority on Victorian housekeeping, Isabella Beeton, was even more thorough. She recommended removing velvet chairs before cleaning the bedroom to avoid harming them with dust. "In bedmaking," she advised, "the fancy of the occupant should be consulted; some like beds sloping from the top towards the feet, swelling slightly in the middle; others perfectly flat." The housemaid was to accommodate the bed to the taste of the sleeper, taking care to shake, beat, and turn it well in the process. Feathers that escaped the featherbed must be replaced inside the tick. Once the lengthy process of laying the bedclothes was complete, "the counterpane is laid over all, which should fall in graceful folds."[17]

The work never stopped and was carefully organized to avoid any "unnecessary bustling and hurrying." One feels sorry for the maids who had to follow Mrs. Beeton's instructions.

A veritable army of servants made Victorian beds fresh and habitable in the interests of cleanliness, health, and a proper and elaborate etiquette. If there were few servants or none at all, the task of keeping a Victorian bedroom clean fell to the housewife. Shirley Forster Murphy, the London County Council's chief health officer in the 1890s, described household dust as "the powder of dried London mud." It included residue from the roads, particles of all kinds of decaying matter, "the droppings of horses and other animals, the entrails of fish . . . the bodies of dead cats, and the miscellaneous contents of dust-bins."[18] Quite apart from this, the hundreds of thousands of houses and commercial buildings in London were almost all heated with coal: coal residue from chimneys was everywhere. Dust and soot blackened everything, to the point that careful householders covered their furniture with covers that were washed regularly. Quite apart from dirtying furniture, airborne dust polluted hairbrushes, which also turned black after even a single hair brushing. The prevalence of all kinds of dirt is almost impossible for westerners to imagine, given today's much cleaner air.

Mattresses were commonly filled with horsehair or, failing that, cow's hair or wool, often laid out above a straw-filled mattress that protected it from the iron frame. By the late nineteenth century many expensive mattresses had chain springs, but even these needed hair padding. If the mattress had no springs, it was covered with sheeting to protect it from the pervasive soot, and a featherbed was often laid atop it, above an under blanket. Such beds were expensive and demanding to maintain.

To prevent the fibers from matting and clumping the mattress had to be turned and shaken daily. An under sheet was tucked into the lowest mattress to keep out soot. Then came a bottom sheet, a top sheet, several blankets—as many as four in cold weather—a bolster, and pillows. The pillows were covered with good quality Dutch sheeting, then with pillowcases. Washing all this bedding was another laborious task. Several writers suggested that blankets be washed (by hand) every other week and sheets about once a month. If two people shared the bed, then the sheets should be washed once every two weeks. To save labor, sheet washing was staggered, the bottom sheet being washed, then the top one becoming the bottom one, while a clean top sheet came into service.

Twice a year, in spring and fall, there was a major overhaul of the entire bedding setup—whence the term "spring cleaning." Another formidable housekeeping expert, Mary Haweis, remarked that fleas were unacceptable in a decent bedroom.[19] Mattresses and pillows were taken outside and aired. Every few years a careful household with servants to do the hard work would take the bedding and mattresses apart, wash them, and sift the feathers to get rid of dust. It was important to check for fleas and other bugs at least once a week. If vermin were found, the bed was disassembled and washed with chloride of lime and water. The bedroom was thoroughly cleaned and disinfected and all openings sealed. If the infestation was truly out of control, the bed would be placed in an empty room that was sealed airtight. Then the homeowner burned sulfur to kill off the pests. As Beatrix Potter of Peter Rabbit fame once observed, one didn't want "too much Natural History in a bed."

All these concerns besides the problem of careless gentlemen who insisted on writing in their bedrooms. Inevitably, accidents happened—ink was spilled, and it was indelible. The offender would unthinkingly grab a towel and mop up the ink, with disastrous results. Mrs. Haweis, known as "an arbiter of fashionable interior decoration," pronounced firmly that gentlemen should be discouraged from using toilet towels to mop up ink and spilled water. She recommended hanging a couple of dusters on a convenient towel horse.

Where would all this end? Sometimes it could get worse. In 1973 the troubled Austrian writer Ingeborg Bachmann died, having set her bed alight. A compulsive pill taker, it seems she fell asleep while smoking. Yet a writer at the beginning of the twentieth century speculated that within a few generations the bedroom would disappear. One would merely go to sleep on the hygienically protected floor of one's library or sitting room. This has not come to pass. The bed and what happens there have always determined the role of the bedroom, whatever distractions appear.

Bedrooms as we know them today are the direct consequence of a craving for a refuge from the hurly-burly of an increasingly industrialized and urban world. Today, they are arguably the most private place in any house (even the family bathroom is semipublic in that it is used by many and, indeed, by visitors). Centered around the bed with its mattress and soft pillows, our bedrooms are ideally places of comfort and serenity. The peace of the private bedroom is one of the greatest legacies of the Victorians. It is now widely found in every corner of the industrialized world and in elite houses the globe over.

Each culture nonetheless brings its own flavor to the bedroom, whether in terms of tastes in decor or in regional ideology. In China, for instance, an interior design penchant for feng shui rules and regulations calls to mind the birth charts of yore. Among the main bedroom prescriptions: do not locate the bed facing the bedroom door; do place the bed head against a wall; do not place the bed diagonally, as this creates negative empty space; do not place the bed under a heavy beam, as this will sap your qi, or personal energy; do not put your bed under a window; do not put the bed against a wall abutting a kitchen or bathroom. Some of these ideas are quite sensible, although sometimes the philosophy verges on the mystical. Thus serious sleepers are advised to take note of their *Kua* number, divined from one's birth date and sex, and to then follow specific charts to decide lucky and unlucky places within the room to actually place the bed. For extra points, your partner's Kua number should be added into the mix. One imagines that after all this mental effort one would indeed sleep pretty soundly.

However the bedroom is arranged, the secluded bedroom is recent, our personal bed is recent, and our time in bed has never been quite so peaceful. Or it would be if, against every recommendation of sleep therapists, we didn't electronically bring the entire world into bed with us.

TEN

Tomorrow's Beds

While the basic design of a bed, this seemingly prosaic piece of furniture, has changed little over the millennia, its functions have varied wildly across time and space. The humble charpoy is witness to this reality: a completely practical, flat sleeping place but with very local cultural manifestations—ideal for moving onto the veranda for ebullient poetry recitals, as favored in Pakistan, or for shifting onto the roof to sleep in the cool night breeze. And when you die, the charpoy might be stood on its end to honor you.[1]

Of all the artifacts that surround us, beds are among the most universal. In the modern West the bed is usually a passive object, tucked in a corner, drawing no comment. But it is what we do with the bed that is interesting. John Lennon and Yoko Ono reminded us of this in 1969 when they turned a hotel bed into a political arena by staging a "bed-in" for peace. They stayed in bed for a week shortly after their marriage, first at the Amsterdam Hilton and then at the Queen Elizabeth, Montreal. They engaged in heated discussions with visitors—a sort of contemporary levée—in their luxurious

John Lennon and Yoko Ono on their peace bed during their honeymoon.

hotel beds, ultimately with an audience of millions. One wonders if they remembered Louis XIV: probably not.

BACK TO THE FUTURE

Futurists have delivered numerous prophecies about the bed, most of which are, at best, fantasies. As Thomas Frey of the DaVinci Institute remarks, "Sexual relationships on a levitating bed would . . . force people to get rather creative."[2] Several decisive trends seem likely to define the relationships between beds and people. Perhaps the most compelling is the uncomfortable reality of ever-rising urban populations and the proliferation of what is euphemistically called high-density housing. This often translates into high-rises—witness the extraordinary urban landscapes of Beijing, Shanghai, New York, or San Francisco—where housing prices and rents are astronomic. People spend their entire lives in tiny apartments. Tens of thousands of city dwellers sleep in their living rooms, with the kitchen, such as it is, a few steps away. Cramped quarters tax the ingenuity of bed and mattress designers as never before.

The kind of trundle beds that rolled under monarchs' four-posters centuries ago are still in routine use. So are sleeper couches, once notoriously uncomfortable but now much improved with better hinges and mattresses. Folding beds, as we have seen, are nothing new. Sears, Roebuck sold "modern" folding beds decades ago, but the grandparent of almost all such modern space-saving devices is the Murphy bed. William Lawrence Murphy was born in California, the son of a forty-niner from the Gold Rush.[3] He broke in horses, drove a stagecoach, and served briefly as sheriff of a small pioneer town. At the turn of the twentieth century he rented a tiny one-room apartment in San Francisco. His bed took up almost all the space. Legend has it that he was wooing an opera singer but could not invite her to his apartment because it was considered immoral for an unmarried woman to enter a man's bedroom. Murphy wanted a folding bed that would become invisible. He used an old closet doorjamb and some door hinges to build a pivot that attached the bed to the wall and allowed it to fold up out of sight. According to his descendants, Murphy married his girlfriend, and her father lent him the money to patent and manufacture what he called the Murphy-In-A-Dor Bed. His new venture was already a success when the 1906 earthquake struck the city. Some of the beds folded up during the quake, killing at least one occupant. At a time when people were flocking to growing cities and housing was crowded and in short supply Murphy beds were a big success as space savers. Sales peaked in the early 1900s, but the same company still manufactures them today.

A Murphy bed in use in an apartment in New York City.

The Murphy bed design does not involve box springs. The mattress lies on a wooden platform or on wire mesh, secured by straps so that it doesn't sag when the bed is closed. The original models folded vertically into the wall, but now you can purchase side-folding Murphys and beds with shelves, tables, or folding desks that appear when the bed disappears into the wall cavity. There are even models that turn into sofas or contain office accessories.

Murphy beds are an ideal solution for people living in condominiums or apartments where space is at a premium, especially since innovations like piston-lifts have made them easier to raise and lower. Proper installation is essential, lest the bed collapse on the operator. A drunk man died in a closed Murphy bed in 1982, and two women were trapped and suffocated by an improperly installed Murphy in 2005. Murphys starred in the Charlie Chaplin movie *One A.M.* (1916) and the James Bond film *You Only Live*

Twice. Bond is trapped in a Murphy, then shot through the bed. It appears he's killed, but of course he's not.

There are other ingenious solutions to the space problem. Some people hang their bed from the apartment ceiling. This may give you a lofty sleeping experience and free up floor space, but the ceiling has to be reinforced and the bed properly installed. Another idea: turn your bed into a storage capsule. You sleep atop a piece of furniture that stores and hangs your clothes, shelves books, and holds your entertainment center. Only single beds are practicable, you need a ladder, and have to be careful not to fall out. But perhaps the future lies with "smart furniture." Ori Living are pioneers of robotic furniture in which entire rooms can be moved around at the touch of a switch, with a smartphone app, or via voice activation methods. Aimed at those living in the aforementioned high-density urban housing, the company's upbeat promo video promises a way to "re-imagine how we live in our spaces . . . multiplying the livability and efficiency of your space."[4] Ori provides the material: entire false walls, closets, cabinets, and other pieces of furniture that slide around magnetic tracks plugged into electrical sockets. Walls push back or close in, making a sofa area appear where before a closet stood. In their Studio Suite, the bed—like some sort of ultimate trundle bed—slides up against a wall and is covered by a desk, transforming the bedroom area into a dining room / party zone. Fear not, Ori assure us that moving furniture will halt if obscured by an object weighing more than a few pounds and it can all be moved by hand in the event of a blackout.

CHANGING SPACES

Some people, including computer programmers and writers, are returning to the home to work. Where space is tight and expensive, and for those unwilling or unable to go robotic, some simply reconfigure their interiors themselves, for example by sleeping above their work desks. Known as loft beds, these are also a favorite in kids' rooms, for children are much more amenable to climbing up to bed than their parents.

The Japanese, who have long lived in small spaces, have for centuries slept on the *shikibuton,* a thin mattress that lives on a shelf during the day and is unrolled on the floor at night. The shikibuton is part of the futon, a Japanese bed set. It serves as the cushion of the set, about four inches (ten centimeters) thick, roughly half that of an American futon, and is stuffed with organic cotton, latex, and wool to form a thick mattress. Shikibutons are intended to be used on the floor and are stowed away every morning. They have the huge advantage of freeing up floor space but provide a firmer sleeping experience than a conventional bed. You need to turn them every two or three weeks to ensure they wear evenly and put them away during the day to prevent mildew from forming under them. You can also buy a foam folding shikibuton, a form of Japanese mattress that is popular in San Francisco.

Others, such as the so-called digital nomads, usually young, wealthy, and tech-savvy westerners, have embraced life on the move. The Dutch architectural practice Studio Makkink and Beyhas has designed a potential bed for this market. Their 2014 Nomadic Living futuristic folding bed uses natural materials, including wood and wool and a great deal of white cotton. Evoking ideas of a former imagined pastoral idyll but without the mud, the bed packs tightly away into a round bundle, allowing its owner to carry it comfortably on his or her back. All these solutions are ways of cramming more bed into less space. Three centuries after the Industrial Revolution began, millions of people—entire families, couples, or just roommates—live in far closer quarters than they did even a couple of generations ago. Such proximity is once again redefining privacy as we've known it since the nineteenth century. Privacy in bed was a given for middle-class folk for generations, but no longer. Apartment dwelling means living up close with family or sometimes with housemates who can be, at any rate initially, strangers. How do you isolate yourself? The answers require more ingenious solutions than noise-canceling earphones. Even people living in conventional bedrooms or in large spaces sometimes crave complete solitude, hard to find in a world where TVs blare and cell phones are virtually universal.

SOUND SLEEP

Judging from magazine articles and the web, we westerners have an almost manic obsession with finding ways to achieve sound sleep, the magical, perhaps mythical eight hours of undisturbed slumber. Much of this quest revolves around pharmaceutical or herbal remedies and advice to abstain from late-night drinking, caffeinated coffee after noon, or eating too much too late. Pillows have also been given a pro-sleep redesign, such as the YourFacePillow, whose bolstered sides aim to keep you settled on your back. But much comes down to the bed and its mattress. The slowly changing bed reflects technological shifts and the ebb and flow of fashion. Most of the innovation has revolved around the mattress, with some fascinating tangents like the demand for waterbeds, very much a "groovy" product of the 1960s.

Waterbeds had been around for much longer than that, with some (sadly) unsubstantiated sources suggesting an ancient Mesopotamian origin. But it was Charles Hall, an industrial design student, and some friends at San Francisco State University who, for Hall's master's thesis, designed a water-filled vinyl mattress.[5] He experimented with 136 kilograms of corn starch gel and even Jell-O, which unfortunately decomposed, before turning to water. After he graduated, Hall called his waterbed the Pleasure Pit and sold it at thirty retail locations throughout California. His early customers included the rock group Jefferson Airplane and the Smothers

Brothers. But as cheap imitations, all of them targeting hippies and swinging singles, flooded the marketplace, Hall was unable to defend his patents. One make was called Wet Dream, its big selling point being sex and the erotic prospect of all kinds of interesting positions. Hugh Hefner commissioned one with a cover made from Tasmanian possum hair. By the 1980s waterbeds went mainstream and were favored by people with bad backs or who were allergic to conventional mattresses. And they became a favorite topic in movies and TV shows, in which they usually exploded or sprang a leak.

By 1987 a remarkable 22 percent of all mattresses sold in the United States were waterbeds. But there were serious disadvantages. Waterbeds were fine if you didn't mind running a hose into your bedroom, with all the attendant risks of a spill while filling the bed or, even worse, a leak while you slept. Draining the bed requires an electric pump; the early ones were very heavy. Many sleepers disliked the squishiness. By the 1990s conventional mattress designers had come up with innovations that made their products lighter, softer, and more flexible. The waterbed market faded rapidly in the face of this competition and became a niche segment. Today, more sophisticated versions have "bladders" that act like large water balloons, wave reduction systems, and temperature control for a warm sleep. Waterbeds can be bought with built-in surround sound, therapeutic lighting, and a mattress that simulates the weightlessness you experience in space. Those who are devoted to waterbeds are passionately loyal, but most people now stay away from them even if they like the feel. Who wants to run a hose through the bedroom window? Hall himself still sleeps on a waterbed at his home on Bainbridge Island, Washington. Much more sophisticated designs are on his mind. He's getting back into the business via a Florida test market with a friend who owns a chain of furniture stores. Maybe it's an idea whose time has come once again with new generations who were not part of the cool revolution of the 1970s.

Mainstream mattress manufacturers operate in a crowded and lucrative marketplace, especially in North America. Some of them are now expanding overseas, arguing, probably correctly, that there are burgeoning markets among well-off sleepers in Asia and elsewhere. The market bristles with variations despite being a seemingly conservative sales pitch. For instance, the well-known Sealy mattress line includes adjustable bases "with a variety of enhanced options." You can order a base that adjusts only the head or invest in a version called the Reflexion 4 that offers a virtually unlimited range of ergonomic positions for the head and feet. All the bases have wireless remotes, and the Reflexion has "dual massage zones." Sealy describes its top-of-the-line Tempur-Pedic mattress as being "exquisitely tailored," combining a silk-cashmere cover with "diamond embossed" side panels.

One wonders what peaks of comfort lie ahead. Very high-end mattresses have become a market unto themselves. Duxiana beds from Sweden have components that give you three firmness layers within the mattress and a lumbar support system that allows you to adjust the amount of support to your lower back. The Swedish Hastens Company has been manufacturing beds for more than 150 years, catering to the ultrawealthy with mattresses that take over three hundred hours to make and hand stitch. They start at $13,000 and can go as high as $140,000. You can customize your bed set with exotic extras—furs, superb fabrics, fine metals, or whatever catches your fancy. All are handmade, with extra detailing unknown in our humbler mattresses. Hastens mattresses are so durable that they are passed down for generations. The slightly less expensive Palais Royal, manufactured by Kluft in California, has thousands of springs wrapped in hand-sewn cotton, two layers of horsehair, and more than ten layers, including 4.5 kg of cashmere from New Zealand. Ten artisans take three days to make your mattress. The English manufacturer Vispring makes entirely custom mattresses, for which you choose the tension and other details as well as the fabrics, possibly even a layer of vicuna wool, which will raise the cost of your mattress to over $71,000. It's said to be incredibly soft and make you feel like you're lying on a cloud.

There comes a point where practical advantages yield to prestige and privilege. A bed is no longer something you flaunt, but those who spend monstrous sums on their sleeping platforms often just want to surround themselves with the best, even if they don't sleep any better as a result. The quest for the perfect mattress will continue unabated, as different manufacturers strive for market share. Apart from the ever-changing internal technologies, much of the innovation in mattresses extends into what one can add to the bed. Increasingly, the bed is becoming a safe haven from the realities of the fast-paced world. Much of the emphasis today is on peace and serenity, on giving people the choice of remaining connected or cutting themselves off completely.

Then there's serenity for your domestic beasts. According to the American Pet Products Association, nearly half of all pet dogs, including 62 percent of small dogs, 41 percent of medium-sized dogs, and 32 percent of large ones, sleep on or in their owners' beds. Sleeping with one's owner gives both cats and dogs a sense of security as well as warmth. For the 50 percent that don't sleep with their owners, dog beds have become a large marketplace. They are regularly sold in online catalogs whose illustrations feature yellow Labradors lounging in decadent comfort. Up-market examples feature memory foam, raised sides, and washable fabrics or covers. There are even "burrow beds," which are almost like sleeping bags, or just simple cushions, and, lest we forget, dog beds for the car. The upscale fishing and outdoor lifestyle outfitter Orvis sells "ToughChew" beds that "know how to take a beating—or a biting." They feature double-layer construction that resists chewing, digging, or shredding. Orvis will give you a full refund if your dog chews through the bed. It is available in a variety of colors, features soft, rugged materials, and can be embroidered with your favorite hound's name.

FUTURE DREAMS

Perhaps the bed of the future is the pod bed: a capsule that satisfies your every need as you loll under the covers. They already exist, but are far from universal. Pod beds have all the necessary computer connections, and they adjust temperature, lighting, and even external sound levels by monitoring the sleeper's comfort level. Naturally, these beds have automatic massage systems that will gently rock the bed and waken you slowly and softly. Canopy pods are equipped with a media screen so that a couple can watch TV or browse the web without getting up. When sleep beckons, press a button and the screen is sealed off by a plain blind.

Some sleeping pods include an entire multimedia entertainment system, complete with game consoles and an HD projector. As might be expected, you can adjust your bed any way you wish, and there are blinds that enclose you for those intimate moments. Or you can have an Ecotypic bed, which comes with its own plants, lit by LEDs to help them grow, speakers that play music to send you to sleep, and even its own power-generating system. Every activity in and around the bed converts into energy. The Cloud, which uses magnetic force to levitate a soft upper cushion, is a good place to relax or sleep but impractical for much else, requiring a rather puritan life.

Bed pods are often associated with capsule hotels, a rapidly expanding segment of the hotel business, especially in Asia. They cater to both business travelers and frugal tourists, who want the basics— a place to sleep, fast Wi-Fi, charging facilities for their electronics, and a small desk, if necessary. Capsule hotels are particularly attractive to young urban travelers, who want accommodation close to the city center and flexibility. There's a premium on convenience, which accounts in large part for the explosive growth in capsule hotels and their simple beds in Asia. Many of them are in rapidly expanding chains, who will even allow one to rent a room by the hour—a popular option for the weary at airports; and, though unspoken, sometimes also for those buying sex.

The earliest capsule hotels originated in Japan as places to stay with no frills and almost no interaction with fellow guests. Now the concept has evolved, with an increasing emphasis on coworking spaces and areas where guests can mingle. You can even Instagram your customized hi-tech pod. There are ingenious niche capsule hotels, like ones in bookstores in Kyoto and Tokyo, where you sleep among the books, tucked away among the shelves. The actual beds are the same as usual, but their environments are more and more custom made and technologically sophisticated, there no longer being one type of bed for everyone.

Pods, canopies, magnetic floaters, and deluxe waterbeds all have one common denominator, connectivity, which was unknown only a few years ago. Some mattresses already have USB ports and Bluetooth. It's only a matter of time before your bed will be fully synced with your smartphone so that you can browse the Internet or virtually chat with others throughout your levée and couchée. All this connects with futuristic technology that allows the bed to know when to raise or lower the temperature or adjust music and light. All you have to do is bask indolently in an ambience created by computer power. Virtual reality could allow your mattress to let you sleep amid flowering blooms, atop the Empire State Building in New York, or under a full moon and stars. In the near future you'll be able to buy a mattress that has customized comfort zones for each occupant with individual heat and air conditioning. Someone will surely develop a holographic companion to read you bedroom stories. We'd personally far rather invest in self-cleaning and bacteria-resistant mattresses that can eliminate bedbugs.

Like our forebears, the sleepers of the future will undoubtedly prefer to recline on a comfortable surface, but the futurists won't leave it alone. Some call levitation the ultimate, envisaging a series of air jets that suspend you in midair. You would be able to dial in the strength of the air jets and float in your version of space. Pillows will be embedded with chips and sensors to measure your vital signs, track sleep patterns, and give you ideal wake-up times. Ceilings and walls will glow with light that can mimic day or night. There's talk of headsets and buds for in-bed smartphones and of voice-controlled and sensor-operated heating and cooling. And in light of high-density living and ever-smaller apartments there's talk of automated furniture which turns a living room into a bedroom. Vertical rooms will become more commonplace, perhaps for sleeping in bags like astronauts. But how will we create the weightlessness that would make such a sleeping bag comfortable?

Most of us lie on mattresses that our grandparents would recognize—except that ours are probably more comfortable. Why add smart technology to the mix? Do we really want electronics to track not only our medical conditions but also our musical tastes, favorite things to read, and buying preferences? For the ever-increasing numbers addicted to their health-monitoring smartwatches and calorie-counting cell phone apps, the answer is probably yes. Soon we'll be able to buy a mattress with a built-in sleep tracker, which will give us not a static bed but one that theoretically will improve over time. There are those who argue that sleep tracking will make you sleep smarter—whatever that means. A mattress may be able to create optimum conditions for sleep, but it won't fix your perceived sleeping problem. For most of us, short of giving up the day job and keeping one's own schedule, a sensible diet, going to bed at a decent hour, exercising regularly, and frolicking with bedfellows are probably the best routes to a sound sleep.

The bed that was once a lively place where all life played out has disappeared into the shadows, but now it promises to become virtually sociable. According to the American artist Laurie Anderson, "Technology is the campfire around which we tell our stories." She's partly right. Through technology we can anticipate being able to bring anyone or any thoughts into our beds—yet without the physical closeness our ancestors took as normal.

Infinitely connected and infinitely detached: today's bed reflects our lives, just as it always has. As we peel back the sheets on tomorrow's bed, we can see the future of our world, with all its atomistic nightmares but also all its interconnected dreams, writ large.

Notes

ONE

Beds Laid Bare

1. Wright, 2004.
2. Samson, 2012.
3. Thoemmes et al, 2018.
4. Wadley et al., 2011.
5. Nadel, 2004.
6. Shafer and Bryant, 1977.
7. Childe, 1983.
8. Richards, 2005; Richards and Jones, 2016.
9. Parker Pearson, 2012.
10. Malone and Stoddart, 2016; Malone, 2008.
11. Tetley, 2000. A useful general account of ground sleeping: "Instinctive sleeping and resting postures: an anthropological and zoological approach to treatment of lower back and joint pain," https://www.ncbi.nlm.nih.gov/pmc/articles/PMC1119282/.
12. Dodson and Hilton, 2004.
13. Reeves, 1990.
14. Siculus, *Historical Library*, vol. 1: chapter 70.
15. Carlano and Sumberg, 2006; Crystal, 2015.

195

16. For the Tristan Quilt, see the Victoria and Albert Museum website: http://collections.vam.ac.uk/item/o98183/the-tristan-quilt-bed-cover-unknown/.
17. https://www.pepysdiary.com/diary/1666/08/15.
18. Ormiston and Wells, 2010.
19. http://www.retailtimes.co.uk/bed-overtakes-sofa-used-piece-furniture-british-homes-made-com-reports/.

TWO
Sleep through Time

1. Sir William Vaughan (c. 1575–1641) was a Welsh writer who promoted colonization in Newfoundland. The quotation is from Vaughan, 1609, chapter 3.
2. Phiston, 1609.
3. Ibid.
4. Cited by Ekirch, 2005: 310.
5. Freud and Strachey, 2010.
6. Horne, 2007: 165.
7. Den Boer, 2012.
8. Wehr, 1992.
9. Ekirch, 2005. For early modern England, see Handley, 2016.
10. Glaskin and Chenhall, 2013.
11. See Yetish et al., 2015.
12. Huffington, 2017: 76.
13. Walker, 2017.
14. Reiss, 2017.
15. Horne, 207.
16. Churchill, 2013: 999.
17. From an interview with Edison by Edward Marshall, *New York Times*, February 6, 1927.
18. Kripke et al., 2002.

THREE
The Big Bang

1. Tacitus, *Annals* 15: 37–41. Emperor Nero (AD 37–68) was an extravagant, tyrannical ruler who committed suicide when he learned he had been condemned to death in absentia as a "public enemy."
2. Crystal, 2015.
3. Booth, 2015.
4. Cooper, 2002: 94.

5. Xenophon, 1979, chapter 7, section 11.
6. Crystal, 2015: 144.
7. Wright, 2004: 72.
8. Tannahill, 1980, chapter 7.
9. Grundy, 2010. See also Patterson, 2013.
10. Malinowski, 1929.
11. George, 2016.
12. Crystal, 2015: 15. British Museum accession number 1867, 0509.55.
13. Tannahill, 1980: 164. See also Van Gulik, 1994.
14. Tannahill, 1980. See chapter 8 for a comprehensive discussion. See also Daniélou, 1993.
15. Straton. From *Anthologica Palantinus*, 12, 4, quoted by Tannahill, 1980: 75.
16. Socrates. From Xenophon, *Symposium* 2, quoted by Tannahill, 1980: 83.
17. Plutarch, "Life of Lycurgus," 18, quoted by Tannahill, 1980: 90.
18. Knudsen, 2012.
19. McGinn, 2004.
20. Wright, 2004: 40.
21. Tannahill, 1980: 381–87.

FOUR

Call the Midwife

1. Scientific analysis of the teeth of the fetus, performed in 2017, revealed that mother and baby died between the thirty-first and thirty-third gestational weeks and that both suffered severe stress during the last two and a half months of life. See Nava et al., 2017, for the full illustrated report.
2. Genesis 3:16.
3. The Seated Woman of Çatalhöyük (with restored head) is on permanent display at the Anatolian Civilizations Museum, Ankara, Turkey (see kultur. gov.tr).
4. For detailed information about current infant mortality rates, see the World Health Organization: http://www.who.int/gho/child_health/mortality/mortality_under_five_text/en/.
5. Papyrus Westcar: www.revolvy.com. For background and discussion, see Booth, 2015, and Blackman, 1988.
6. Nunn, 2002.
7. Sushruta or Susruta, called the Father of Surgery, was born around 600 BC in Uttar Pradesh, India. His treatise *The Compendium of Sushruta* is one of the most important surviving ancient texts on medicine. See Bhishagratna, 2006.
8. King, 2005; Soranus of Ephesus and Owsei Temkin, 1991.

9. Posidippus, as quoted by Blundell, 1995: 131. Posidippus was an epigraphic poet of the second century BC.
10. Cook and Luo, 2017.
11. From *Ishinpo*, 23.8 a. *Ishinpo*, thirty volumes long and the oldest surviving Japanese medical text, was completed in AD 984 by Ramba Yasuyori. As quoted by Jen-der Lee, 1996: 228.
12. From Wang Tao, quoting from the work of Cui Zhiti (d. AD 681), who wrote widely on childbirth medicine. As quoted by Jen-der Lee, 1996: 235.
13. This saying comes from *Ishinpo*, 23.24a, as quoted by Jen-der Lee, 1996: 234.
14. Licence, 2012: 213.
15. As detailed by the botanic gardens at Kew, London (kew.org).
16. Licence, 2012: 213.
17. From a study by Roger Schofield, 1993. "Did the mothers really die?" in Peter Laslett, ed., *The World We Have Lost* (Cambridge: Cambridge University Press), cited by Licence, 2012.
18. François Mauriceau (1637–1709) was a leading seventeenth-century obstetrician. Quotation in Mauriceau, 1668: 157.
19. Meigs, 1854: 104. Charles Delucena Meigs (1792–1869) was an American obstetrician who opposed obstetrical anesthesia and believed physicians' hands could not possibly transmit disease.
20. Kleeman, 2015.

FIVE

Death and Beyond

1. El Brujo is a complex of ceremonial structures built by the Moche state of coastal Peru between AD 1 and 600. The Lady of Cao remains unpublished in detail, except for popular accounts, including a feature by Nadia Durrani in *Current World Archaeology* (2009, issue 35): see https://www.world-archaeology.com/travel/moche-route-the/.
2. Quotation from Tablet 8 of the Epic of Gilgamesh, fully searchable online at http://www.ancienttexts.org/library/mesopotamian/gilgamesh/tab8.htm. Or see also George, 2016.
3. Baughan, 2013, chapters 1, 2.
4. Reisner, 1923.
5. Kemp et al., 2013.
6. Bianucci et al., 2015.
7. Reeves, 1990.
8. The contents of Kha's tomb are on display at the refurbished Museo Egizio (Egyptian museum) in Turin, Italy. See https://www.museoegizio.it/en/.

9. Tomb H18 was published by the archaeologist Kathleen Kenyon, the excavator of Jericho, in 1960 and is cited by Baughan, 2013.
10. Baughan, 2013.
11. Needham and Ping-Yü, 1959, 1970.
12. Whitelock, 2013: 338ff.
13. Quoted in ibid., 342.
14. Ibid.
15. Plato (born in the mid to late 420s BC) recorded Socrates's death (in 399 BC) in *Phaedo*, also known to ancient readers as "On the Soul." Text translated by Benjamin Jowett (1892), quotation from 113.
16. Tacitus was born around AD 56–57, when Nero was emperor. Quotation from *Annals*, book 15: 60–64. See Blakeney, 1908, 1:498–502. For Seneca's death, see Ker, 2009.
17. Nimoy's tweet can be found here: https://twitter.com/therealnimoy/status/56 9762773204217857?lang=en.
18. Steenkamp was Pistorius's girlfriend. Pistorius was convicted of murdering her in 2013. Her tweet is here: https://twitter.com/reevasteenkamp?lang=en.
19. Hardy, 1998: 117.
20. For footage of the Torajans, see http://www.bbc.co.uk/news/magazine-39603771.

SIX
Strange Bedfellows

1. The Great Bed of Ware can be seen at the Victoria and Albert Museum, London, Room 57. See www.vam.ac.uk. Prince Ludwig I of Anhalt-Köthen (1579–1650) was also an unexceptional princeling who preferred agricultural development to making war. Quote from www.greatbedofware.org.uk.
2. Shakespeare, *Twelfth Night* 3:2.
3. Quotations from www.greatbedofware.org.uk.
4. Ekirch, 2005: 279. See also Worsley, 2012.
5. Melville, 2012: 36.
6. Butterfield, 1961: 418.
7. Liedloff, 1975: 17.
8. John Whiting (1908–91) and his wife, Beatrice Whiting (1914–2004), were leading psychological anthropologists who pioneered the comparative study of child development, first at Yale and then at Harvard. See Edwards and Bloch (2010) for an overview of their work, and Pawlik and Rosenzweig, 2000: 242, for more on the research cited here.
9. Carlano and Sumburg, 2006: 83.
10. Handley, 2016.

11. Ekirch, 2005.
12. Ibid.
13. Tomalin, 2007.
14. Tahhan, 2013.
15. From *The Works of Benjamin Jonson* (London, 1616), quoted by Ekirch 2005: 292.
16. Soranus and Temkin, 1991. See also Soranos, *Gynaikia* (P. Burguière, D. Gourévitch, and Y. Malinas, trans. and eds., *Soranus d'Ephèse: maladies des femmes* [Paris 1988], 1:xxxix–xl).
17. For James McKenna's work, see https://cosleeping.nd.edu.
18. Ibid.
19. Carlona and Sumberg, 2006, chapter 7. Wright, 2004, chapter 33.
20. Carlona and Sumberg, 2006.
21. Borel, 2015.
22. Gizelle Schoch, personal communication.
23. Reiss, 2017.

SEVEN

The Moving Bed

1. Lorenzi, 2017.
2. Lehner and Hawass, 2017.
3. Quotations from Fagles, 1996: book 4, ll. 332–35, and book 20, l. 410.
4. Thesiger and Anderson, 2008.
5. Lattimore, 1941.
6. Richardson, 2014.
7. The Englishman John Evelyn was a writer on many topics, including horticulture, theology, and vegetarianism. He kept his *Diary* (some parts are more like a memoir in that they were added much later) from 1640 to 1706. Quotation from Bédoyère, 1995: 63.
8. Ibn Battuta. 1853–58, 3:380.
9. George Robert Gleig (1796–1888) was a soldier who became a priest. He wrote numerous books on military topics, including a biography of Wellington. Quotation from Gleig, 1871: 127.
10. Information on Napoleon's camp bed is from Fondation Napoleon at Napoleon.org. HomeHistory of the Two EmpiresObjectsNapoleon's camp bed.
11. Quotations in this paragraph from Miller, 1915: 62.
12. Startzman, 2014.
13. Frink and Frink, 1897: 7.
14. Richardson and Eberlein, 1925.

15. Leyendecker, 1992.
16. Discussion of RVs is in Jim Morrison, "Commemorating 100 Years of the RV," www.Smithsonianmag.com, August 24, 2010.

EIGHT

The Public Bedchamber

1. Wright, 2004: 29.
2. Ibid.
3. Big marital beds: ibid., 73.
4. Whitelock, 2013.
5. Ibid., 244.
6. Mitford and Mansel, 2012.
7. Siculus, 2014: vol. 1: chapter 70.
8. The Duke of Saint-Simon (1675–1755) was a soldier, writer, and unrivaled, if unreliable, chronicler of King Louis XIV's court. Saint-Simon's *The Memoirs of Louis XIV* is a major source on Versailles. See https://www.gutenberg.org/files/3875/3875-h/3875-h.htm.
9. Wright, 2004: 108.
10. Saddiq Muhammed Khan Abassi IV's bed is known from a watercolor and several 1882 photographs taken by Christofle. See Skoggard, 2000.
11. Danchev and Todman, 2001: 223.

NINE

A Private Refuge

1. Comment made at a Federal Trade Commission workshop on the Internet of Things in 2013.
2. Malinowski, 1929.
3. Pliny the Elder, *Natural History*, book 35. Pliny and Holland, 2013.
4. Pompeii graffiti: McGinn, 2004.
5. Quotations in this paragraph are from Fagan, 2004: 18–23.
6. Olsen, 1976.
7. Tosh, 1999.
8. Flanders, 2003, introduction and chapter 1.
9. From the June 1918 edition of *Earnshaw's Infants' Department*, a trade publication.
10. Warren and Brandeis, 1890: 196.
11. Flanders, 2003, chapter 1.
12. Quoted by Ekirch, 2005: 282.

13. Panton, 1888: 182.
14. Ibid., 183.
15. Ibid., 189.
16. Ibid., 140.
17. Beeton, 1859–61: 992.
18. Flanders, 2003: 47.
19. Haweis, 1889.

TEN
Tomorrow's Beds

1. Charpoys: www.stringbedco.com.
2. Frey, 2016: 65.
3. The best summary of Murphy's life is at https://www.en.wikipedia.org/wiki/Murphy_bed.
4. https://oriliving.com.
5. Greenfield, 2010.

Bibliography

We consulted hundreds of articles, books, and websites for this book, many of them obscure. Only the major sources are listed here. An interested reader will find that the bibliographies in many of the works listed will lead to more specialized literature. Unless otherwise stated, quotations are from publications dealing with the subject listed below.

Baughan, Elizabeth P. 2013. *Couched in Death: Klinai and Identity in Anatolia and Beyond*. Madison: University of Wisconsin Press.

Beard, Mary. *Guardian* article: https://www.theguardian.com/books/2009/mar/2/philosophy.

Bédoyère, Guy de la, ed. 1995. *Diary: John Evelyn*. Woodbridge, UK: Boydell Press.

Beeton, Isabella. 1859–61. *Mrs Beeton's Book of Household Management*. London: Chancellor Press, 1982.

Bhishagratna, Kaviraj Kunjalal, trans. 2006. *The Sushruta Samhita: An English Translation Based on Original Texts*. New Delhi: Cosmo Publications.

Bianucci, Raffaella, et al. 2015. "Shedding New Light on the 18th Dynasty Mummies of the Royal Architect Kha and His Spouse Merit." PLOS One DOI: 10.1371/journal.pone.0131916.

Blackman, A. V. 1988. *The Story of King Cheops and the Magicians*. Hemet, CA: J. V. Books.

Bibliography

Blakeney, E. H., ed. *Tacitus: The Annals*. Vol. 1:498–502. London: J. M. Dent.

Blundell, Sue. 1995. *Women in Ancient Greece*. Cambridge: Harvard University Press.

Booth, Charlotte. 2015. *In Bed with the Ancient Egyptians*. Amberley, UK: Stroud.

Borel, Brooke. 2015. *Infested: How the Beg Bug Infiltrated Our Bedrooms and Took Over the World*. Chicago: University of Chicago Press.

Butterfield. L. H. 1961. *Diary and Autobiography of John Adams*. Vol. 3 Cambridge, MA: Belknap Press.

Carlano, Annie, and Bobbie Sumberg. 2006. *Sleeping Around: The Bed from Antiquity to Now*. Seattle: University of Washington Press; Santa Fe: Museum of International Folk Art.

Childe, Vere Gordon. 1983. *Skara Brae*. Rev. ed. London: HM Stationery Office.

Churchill, Winston S. 2013. *Churchill by Himself*. London: Rosetta Books.

Cook, Constance, and Xinhui Luo. 2017. *Birth in Ancient China: A Study of Metaphor and Cultural Identity in Pre-Imperial China*. Albany: State University of New York Press.

Cooper, Jerold S. 2002. "Virginity in Ancient Mesopotamia." In *Sex and Gender in the Ancient Near East*, ed. S. Parpola and R. Whiting. Helsinki: SAA.

Crystal, Paul. 2015. *In Bed with the Romans*. Amberley, UK: Stroud.

Danchev, Alex, and Daniel Todman, eds. 2001. *Field Marshall Lord Alanbrooke: War Diaries, 1939–1945*. London: Weidenfeld and Nicholson.

Daniélou, Alain. 1993. *The Complete Kama Sutra*. New York: Simon and Schuster.

den Boer, E. 2012. "Spirit Conception: Dreams in Aboriginal Australia." *Dreaming* 22, no. 3: 192–211.

Dodson, Aidan, and Dyan Hilton. 2004. *The Complete Royal Families of Egypt*. London: Thames and Hudson.

Edwards, Carolyn P., and Marianne Bloch. 2010. "The Whitings' Concepts of Culture and How They Have Fared in Contemporary Psychology and Anthropology." Faculty Publications, Department of Psychology. 501. http://digitalcommons.unl.edu/psychfacpub/501.

Ekirch, Roger A. 2005. *At Day's Close: The Night in Times Past*. New York: Norton.

Elyot, Thomas. 1539. *The Castell of Helth*. London: Thomas Bethelet.

Fagan, Brian. 2004. *Fish on Friday: Feasting, Fasting, and the Discovery of the New World*. New York: Basic Books.

Fagles, Robert. 1996. *The Odyssey: Homer*. New York: Viking.

Flanders, Judith. 2003. *Inside the Victorian Home: A Portrait of Domestics Life in Victorian England*. New York: Norton.

Freud, Sigmund, and James Strachey, trans. 2010. *The Interpretation of Dreams: The Complete and Definitive Text*. New York: Basic Books.

Frey, Thomas. 2016. *Epiphany Z: Eight Radical Visions for Transforming Your Future.* Hampton, VA: Morgan James.

Frink, Ledyard, and Margaret A. Frink. 1897. *Journal of a Party of California Gold Seekers.* Oakland, CA: publisher unknown.

George, Andrew. 2016. *The Epic of Gilgamesh.* Rev. ed. New York: Penguin Classics.

Glaskin, Katie, and Richard Chenhall, eds. 2013. *Sleep Around the World: Anthropological Perspectives.* New York: Palgrave Macmillan.

Gleig, George Robert. 1871. *The Life of Arthur, Duke of Wellington.* London: Longmans, Green, Reader, and Dyer.

Goodman, Ruth. 2017. *How to Be a Tudor.* New York: Liveright.

Greenfield, Rebecca. 2010. "The Rise and Fall of the (Sexy, Icky, Practical) Waterbed." *Atlantic,* August 13, 2010.

Grundy, Mrs. 2010. *A History of Four Centuries of Morals in Great Britain and the United States Intended to Illuminate Present Problems.* Reprint. Whitefish, MT: Kessinger.

Handley, Sasha. 2016. *Sleep in Early Modern England.* New Haven: Yale University Press.

Hardy, Thomas. 1998 (1891). *Tess of the d'Urbervilles.* Edited by John Paul Riquelme. New York: Bedford Books.

Haweis, Mary Eliza Joy. 1889. *The Art of Housekeeping.* London: Chatto and Windus.

Horne, Jim. 2007. *Sleepfaring: The Secrets and Science of a Good Night's Sleep.* Oxford: Oxford University Press.

Huffington, Arianna. 2017. *The Sleep Revolution: Transforming Your Life, One Night at a Time.* New York: Harmony Books.

Ibn Battuta. 1853–58. *The Travels of Ibn Battutah.* Translated by Tim Macintosh-Smith. New York: Pan Macmillan.

James, H. E. M. 1888. *The Long White Mountain, or a Journey in Manchuria.* London: Longmans, Green, 1888.

Ker, James. 2009. *The Deaths of Seneca.* Oxford: Oxford University Press.

Kemp, Barry, et al. 2013. "Life, Death and beyond in Akhenaten's Egypt: Excavating the South Tombs Cemetery at Amarna." *Antiquity* 87, no. 335: 64–78.

King, Helen. 2005. *Greek and Roman Medicine.* Bristol, UK: Bristol Classical Press.

Kleeman, Alexandra. 2015. "The Bed-Rest Hoax: The Case against a Venerable Pregnancy Treatment." *Harper's Magazine.* December, 2015.

Knudsen, Christian D. 2012. "Naughty Nuns and Promiscuous Monks: Monastic Sexual Misconduct in Late Medieval England." PhD diss., University of Toronto.

Kripke, D. F, et al. 2002. "Mortality Associated with Sleep Duration and Insomnia." *Arch Gen Psychiatry* 59, no. 2: 131–36.

Lattimore, Owen. 1941. *Mongol Journeys.* London: Jonathan Cape.

Lee, Jen-der, 1996. "Childbirth in Early Imperial China." *Bulletin of the Institute of History and Philology, Academia Sinica* 67, no. 3: 533–642. Translated by Sabine Wilms, 2005. Available online at www.brill.nl.

Le Goff, Jacques. 2009. *Saint Louis.* Notre Dame, IN: University of Notre Dame Press.

Lehner, Mark, and Zahi Hawass. 2017. *Giza and the Pyramids.* London: Thames and Hudson.

Leyendecker, Liston Edgington. 1992. *Palace Car Prince: A Biography of George Mortimer Pullman.* Boulder: University Press of Colorado.

Licence, Amy. 2012. *In Bed with the Tudors.* Stroud, UK: Amberley.

Liedloff, Jean. 1975. *The Continuum Concept: In Search of Happiness Lost.* New York: Da Capo Press.

Lorenzi, Rossella. 2017. "Fit for a King: Tut's Camping Bed Was an Ancient Marvel." *Live Science,* August 1, 2017. Livescience.com.

Malinowski, Bronislaw. 1929. *The Sexual Life of Savages in North-western Melanesia, British New Guinea.* London: Eugenics.

Malone, C., and S. Stoddart. 2016. "Figurines of Malta." In *The Oxford Handbook of Prehistoric Figurines,* ed. T. Insoll, 729–53. Oxford: Oxford University Press.

Malone, C. A. T. 2008. "Metaphor and Maltese Art: Explorations in the Temple Period." *Journal of Mediterranean Archaeology* 21, no. 1: 81–108.

Marshall, Edward, February 6, 1927. "Edison at 80 views a world he changed." *New York Times* archives.

Mauriceau, Francis. 1668. *The Diseases of Women with Child, and in Child-Bed.* Translated by Hugh Chamberlen. London: T. Cox.

McGinn, Thomas A. J. 2004. *The Economy of Prostitution in the Roman World.* Ann Arbor: University of Michigan Press.

Meigs, Charles. 1854. *On the Nature, Signs and Treatment of Childbed Fevers.* Philadelphia: Blanchard and Lea.

Melville, Herman. 2012 (1851). *Moby-Dick.* New York: Dover Publications.

Miller, Warren Hastings. 1915. *Camp Craft.* Reprint. Kolkata: Ananda Quinn.

Mitford, Nancy, and Philip Mansel. 2012. *The Sun King.* New York: NYRB Classics.

Nadel, Dani. 2004. "Continuity and Change: The Ohalo II and the Natufian Dwelling Structures (Jordan Valley, Israel)." In *The Last Hunter-Gatherers in the Near East,* ed. C. Delage, 75–84. Oxford: BAR International Series.

Naughan, Elizabeth P. 2013. *Couched in Death.* Madison: University of Wisconsin Press.

Nava, Alessia, et al. 2017. "Virtual Histological Assessment of the Prenatal Life History and Age at Death of the Upper Paleolithic Fetus from Ostuni (Italy)." Nature.com Scientific Reports, 7, Article number: 9527.

Needham, Joseph, and Ho Ping-Yü. (1959). "Elixir Poisoning in Medieval China." *Janus* 48: 221–51. Reprinted in *Clerks and Craftsmen in China and the West: Lectures and Addresses on the History of Science and Technology*, 316–39. Cambridge: Cambridge University Press, 1970.

Nunn, John Francis. 2002. *Ancient Egyptian Medicine*. Norman: University of Oklahoma Press.

Olsen, Donald J. 1976. *The Growth of Victorian London*. New York: Penguin.

Ormiston, Rosalind, and Nicholas W. Wells. 2010. *William Morris: Artist, Craftsman, Pioneer*. Rev. ed. London: Flame Tree.

Panton, Jane Ellen. 1888. *From Kitchen to Garrett: Hints for Young Householders*. London: Ward and Downey.

Parker Pearson, Mike. 2012. *Stonehenge: Exploring the Greatest Stone Age Mystery*. London: Simon and Schuster.

Patterson, Anthony. 2013. *Mrs Grundy's Enemies: Censorship, Realist Fiction and the Politics of Sexual Representation*. Bern, Switzerland: Peter Lang.

Pawlik, Kurt, and Mark R Rosenzweig, eds. 2000. *The International Handbook of Psychology*. London: SAGE.

Pepys, Samuel, and Mynors Bright. 1970. *The Diary of Samuel Pepys: A New and Complete Transcription*. Berkeley: University of California Press.

Phiston, William. 1609. *The Schoole of Good Manners, or A New Schoole of Vertue*. London: W. White for William Inoes.

Plato. *Phaedo*. Translated by Benjamin Jowett, 1892. Reissued by CreateSPace Independent Publishing Platform, 2017.

Pliny the Elder. 2013 (AD 77). *Pliny's Natural History: In Thirty-Seven Books*, ed. Philemon Holland. Seattle: Amazon Digital Services.

Reeves, Nicholas. 1990. *The Complete Tutankhamun*. London: Thames and Hudson.

Reisner, George. 1923. *Excavations at Kerma*. Cambridge: Peabody Museum, Harvard University).

Reiss, Benjamin. 2017. *Wild Nights: How Taming Sleep Created Our Restless World*. New York: Basic Books.

Richards, Colin, ed. 2005. *Dwelling among the Monuments*. Cambridge: MacDonald Institute.

Richards, Colin, and Richard Jones, eds. 2016. *The Development of Neolithic House Societies in Orkney*. Oxford: Oxbow Books.

Richardson, A. E., and H. Donaldson Eberlein. 1925. *The English Inn Past and Present*. London: Batsford.

Richardson, Glen. 2014. *The Field of the Cloth of Gold*. New Haven: Yale University Press.

Saint-Simon de Rouvroy, Louis. 1910. *Memoirs of Louis XIV and His Court and of the Regency*. New York: C. F. Collier.

Samson, Donald R. 2012. "The Chimpanzee Nest Quantified: Morphology and Ecology of Arboreal Sleeping Platforms within the Dry Habitat Site of Toro-Semiliki Wildlife Reserve, Uganda." *Primates* 53: 357–64.

Shafer, Harry J., and Vaughn M. Bryant Jr. 1977. *Archaeological and Botanical Studies at Hinds Cave, Val Verde County, Texas*. College Station: Texas A&M University, Anthropological Laboratory, Special Series 1.

Siculus, Diodorus. 2014. *Historical Library*. Translated by Giles Lauren. Seattle: Amazon Digital Services.

Skoggard, Carl A. 2000. "Asleep with Painted Ladies." *Nest* 10: 100–105.

Soranus of Ephesus. 1991. *Soranus' Gynecology*. Translated by Owsei Temkin. Baltimore: Johns Hopkins University Press.

Speert, Harold. 2004. *Obstetrics and Gynecology: A History and Iconography*. 3rd ed. Boca Raton, FL: CRC Press.

Startzman, Ethan. 2014. "A Brief History of Sleeping Bags." ezinearticles.com, January 21, 2014.

Szpakowska, Kasla, and John Baines. 2006. *Through a Glass Darkly: Magic, Dreams, and Prophecy in Ancient Egypt*. Swansea, UK: Classical Press of Wales.

Tahhan, Diana Adis. 2013. "Sensuous Connections in Sleep: Feelings of Security and Interdependency in Japanese Sleep Rituals." In *Sleep around the World: Anthropological Perspectives*, ed. Katie Glaskin and Richard Chenhall, 61–78. New York: Palgrave Macmillan.

Tannahill, Reay. 1980. *Sex in History*. New York: Stein and Day.

Tetley, Michael. 2000. "Instinctive Sleeping and Resting Postures: An Anthropological and Zoological Approach to Treatment of Lower Back and Joint Pain." *British Medical Journal* 321: 1616.

Thesiger, Wilfred, and John Lee Anderson. 2008. *The March Arabs*. Reprint. Baltimore: Penguin Classics.

Thoemmes, Megan S., et al. 2018. "Ecology of Sleeping: The Microbial and Arthropod Associates of Chimpanzee Beds." *Royal Society Open Science* 5, no. 5: 180382 DOI: 10.1098/rsos.180382

Tomalin, Claire. 2007. *Samuel Pepys: The Unequalled Self*. New York: Vintage.

Tosh, John. 1999. *A Man's Place: Masculinity and the Middle-Class Home in Victorian England*. New Haven: Yale University Press.

Van Gulik, Robert H. 1994. *Sexual Life in Ancient China: A Preliminary Survey of Chinese Sex and Society from ca. 1500 B.C. till 1644 A.D.* Leiden: Brill.

Van Meilj, Toon. 2013. "Maori Collective Sleeping as Cultural Resistance." In *Sleep around the World: Anthropological Perspectives,* ed. Katie Glaskin and Richard Chenhall, 133–50. New York: Palgrave Macmillan.

Vaughan, William. 1609. *Approved Directions for Health, Both Natural and Artificiall.* London: T. Snodham for Roger Jackson.

Wadley, Lyn, et al. 2011. "Middle Stone Age Bedding Construction and Settlement Patterns at Sibudu, South Africa." *Science* 334: 6061.

Walker, Matthew. 2017. *Why We Sleep.* New York: Simon and Schuster.

Warren, Samuel D., and Louis D. Brandeis. 1890. "The Right to Privacy." *Harvard Law Review* 4, no. 5: 193–220.

Wehr, Thomas. 1992. "In Short Photoperiods, Human Sleep Is Biphasic." *Journal of Sleep Research* 1, no. 2: 103–7.

Whitelock, Anna. 2013. *Elizabeth's Bed: An Intimate History of Elizabeth's Court.* New York: Picador.

Whiting, John, and Eleanor Hollenberg Chasdi, eds. 2006. *Culture and Human Development: The Selected Papers of John Whiting.* Cambridge: Cambridge University Press.

Wilkinson, Richard. 2017. *Louis XIV.* Abingdon, UK: Routledge.

Worsley, Lucy. 2012. *If Walls Could Talk: An Intimate History of the Home.* New York: Bloomsbury.

Wright, Lawrence. 2004. *Warm and Snug: The History of the Bed.* Stroud, UK: Sutton Books.

Xenophon. 1979. *Xenophon in Seven Volumes.* Vol. 4. Cambridge: Harvard University Press.

Yetish, Gandhi, et al. 2015. "Natural Sleep and Its Seasonal Variations in Three Pre-industrial Societies." *Current Biology* 25, no. 21: 2862–68.

Acknowledgments

Never in our wildest dreams did we imagine that we, as archaeologists, would write a book about beds, the piece of furniture in which we spend a third of our lives! Indeed, once we got going the book transformed from a survey of the artifact itself to a whole history of what we did while in that object.

An unusual set of circumstances led to what has proved to be a challenging and fascinating book. Its seed was sown when Brian was asked to deliver a talk on the history of beds to a small meeting of executives from the Serta and Simmons mattress companies, which were in the process of merging. On hearing this, Bill Frucht at Yale persuaded him to write a book on the topic, at which point Brian asked his friend and writing colleague Nadia Durrani to join as coauthor.

Our thanks are many. Brian is deeply grateful to Chris Cooper and Mary Larson of Mobilis Strategic Advisors Inc. in Montreal, who originally brought him into their consultancy team for the Serta and Simmons project, for affording this opportunity and for their advice. From us both, Bill Frucht at Yale University Press has been a constant source of encouragement, as has Shelly Lowenkopf, who provided invaluable suggestions, while the copy editor Lawrence Kenney has been a joy to work with at the final stage. We're grateful to large numbers of friends and colleagues for comments, ideas, and suggestions, so many in fact that we're unable to thank them all individually. Please accept a collective thank you! Special thanks are due to Aidan Dodson, John Herbert, Matthew Hillier, Caroline Malone, George Michaels, Ortrun Peyn, Samina Riaz, Vernon Scarborough, and Kathleen Sharp.

Finally, heartfelt thanks to our families, who endured our absences as we completed the long process of creating this book. Without them it would never have happened. Thank you all, not forgetting the Great Cat, Atticus Catticus Catamore Moose.

Index

Page numbers in italics indicate illustrations.

Illustration Credits

p. ii, My Bed, Tracey Emin. Tate Modern, London, 1999. Paul Quayle/Alamy Stock Photo.

p. 15, A house at Skara Brae, Orkney Islands, Scotland, with putative stone bed enclosures to right and left. Vincenzo Iacovoni/Alamy Stock Photo.

p. 19, The so-called sleeping woman of Hal Saflieni, Malta, c. 3000 BC. Heritage Image Partnership Ltd/Alamy Stock Photo.

p. 23, Tutankhamun's funerary beds in the antechamber of his tomb, 1922. Jan Walters/Alamy Stock Photo.

p. 63, An erotic mural from the Lupanare, Pompeii. VPC Travel Photo/Alamy Stock Photo.

p. 79, A woman giving birth in the eighteenth century. Chronicle/Alamy Stock Photo.

p. 96, A Christian deathbed in full flow. The demise of Reverend John Wesley. A lithograph from c. 1840. Archive Images/Alamy Stock Photo.

p. 105, The Great Bed of Ware, exhibited in the Victoria and Albert Museum, London. Artokoloro Quint Lox Limited/Alamy Stock Photo.

p. 114, Girls in Bed Room. Two Japanese girls sleeping on a mat, a photograph by Kusakabe Kimbei. Chronicle/Alamy Stock Photo.

p. 126, Tutankhamun's three-part camp bed. © Griffith Institute, University of Oxford.

p. 130, An old man in Rajastan, India, relaxes on a coir-fiber charpoy, a portable bed with legs and a woven sleeping platform. Dinodia Photos/Alamy Stock Photo.

p. 131, Modern-day museum exhibit of Napoleon's camp bed and bedroom/study at his headquarters on the eve of the Battle of Waterloo, 1815. Arterra Picture Library/Alamy Stock Photo.

p. 154, King Louis XIV's bed at Versailles. Norimages/Alamy Stock Photo.

p. 174, An 1886 advertisement for Maple of London's bedroom furniture, including a white bedroom suite and "iron and brass four-post bedsteads." Chronicle/Alamy Stock Photo.

p. 181, John Lennon and Yoko Ono on their peace bed during their honeymoon. Keystone Pictures USA/Alamy Stock Photo.

p. 183, A Murphy bed in use in an apartment in New York City. Patti McConville/Alamy Stock Photo.